Endorsements for

"*Turning Point Moments* is an important book for our times. It offers powerful and insightful stories of people from all walks of life about how they navigated challenges and came out the other side better than before."
~ Marci Shimoff, #1 *NY Times* Bestselling Author, *Happy for No Reason* and *Chicken Soup for the Woman's Soul*

"The world is ripe for *Turning Point Moments!* This book speaks to these times of challenge in all areas of our lives. Real people who have navigated through dark times show you how to take the path of healing, hope, and new possibilities."
~ Lori Leyden, PhD, MBA, Developer of The Grace Process®, Founder of Create Global Healing

"*Turning Point Moments* is a collection of gripping, personal stories reminding us that life's challenges can be a gateway to transformation and resiliency. This is a must-read awakening for those of us who desire fulfilling possibilities in our lives!"
~ Austin Rees, IBCLC, LMT, Owner/Founder Nourish and Align

"The world needs more people to shine their light and to help others do the same. This book does exactly that. It's raw, vulnerable, and powerful and worth the read."
~ Jill Lublin, Four-time Bestselling Author and Master Publicity Strategist

"A graceful reminder that life is a dance between choice and surrender, and that both are necessary for a better future."
~ Lauren Mudrock, Transformational Photographer

"*Turning Point Moments* provides you with the courage and inspiration to step out and be who you were born to be! A must-read book, where every chapter reveals the hope, the strength, and the power inside all of us waiting to be set free!"

~ Erica Nitti Becker, Author, *Mastery: The Art Of Living On Purpose*

"Just when you think that you have no more fight, the stories in *Turning Point Moments* give hope and provide the reader with a starting point to try and understand their own grief, to help recognize that we *grow through* what we *go through*. It is truly an inspirational read."

~ Leahanne Prolas, Psychotherapist

"Now is the perfect time to recognize that our *Turning Point Moments* can be the most empowering door to our own awakening. They offer us the possibility that the gift within the most challenging chapters of life can lead to an unimaginable, extraordinary journey. These stories are a guiding light on that journey."

~ Dr. Angela Marick, Author, *Beauty in the Brokenness*

"In this fast-paced world where people don't have time to reflect on what is happening around them, *Turning Point Moments* is the guide that provides incredible stories that offer a deeper understanding of life and its realities."

~ Nelton Attzs, BSc, MFA, CIAM, PMP

"Turning points in life are like data points—ready to inspire the curious minds of those who are open and ready to receive! This book is a must-read."

~ Rosemarie Smith, Data Analyst

"I have always been a lover of personal stories. Hearing the stories of others is, in my experience, the truest and simplest medicine for the soul. This book is just that, soul medicine for the part of yourself that is yearning for words of wisdom, inspiration, and the enlightenment that are *Turning Point Moments*."

~ Sara Goff, IBCLC

"We are standing at the precipice of epic change forces. Navigating change through the lens of revolutionary thinking and ways of being is revealed through the real-life stories in *Turning Point Moments*. This book is a one-of-a-kind, must-read book that unlocks the gate for humans to understand how to seize life's challenges and utilize the paradox as an opportunity prism that makes us unstoppable."

~ Kathleen Miller, EdD, Next Level Leadership

"*Turning Point Moments* is a collection of real life journeys creating a pathway to realising what is possible in our own lives! Each story is a potential waiting to be explored!"

~ Cindy Mathers, Transformational Leader, Growing Wellbeing

TURNING
POINT
MOMENTS

*True
Inspirational
Stories About
Creating a Life
That Works
for You*

COMPILED BY
CHRISTINE KLOSER

Capucia LLC
211 Pauline Drive #513
York, PA 17402

www.capuciapublishing.com

Send questions to: support@capuciapublishing.com

Paperback ISBN: 978-1-954920-28-6
eBook ISBN: 978-1-954920-29-3
Library of Congress Control Number: 2022910589

Cover Design: fingerplus | Agus Budiyono
Layout: Ranilo Cabo
Editor and Proofreader: Karen W. Burton
Book Midwife: Karen Everitt

Printed in the United States of America

Capucia LLC is proud to be a part of the Tree Neutral® program. Tree Neutral offsets the number of trees consumed in the production and printing of this book by taking proactive steps such as planting trees in direct proportion to the number of trees used to print books. To learn more about Tree Neutral, please visit treeneutral.com.

100% of all publisher proceeds from the sale of this book will go toward supporting people who are experiencing turning point moments in their life through contributions to organizations like Pandemic of Love, The Teen Project, and National Alliance on Mental Health.

To everyone who has ever experienced a turning point
moment in their life

CONTENTS

Contents

INTRODUCTION

The turning point in the life of those who succeed usually comes
at the moment of some crisis.
—Napoleon Hill

Thank you for following the nudge in your heart to pick up this book and crack open the cover. My guess is—like the contributing authors—you understand the significance of turning point moments in your life.

Perhaps as you read this, you're in the middle of one of those gut-wrenching turning points, or you've just come through a challenging situation with a renewed sense of faith and hope. Perhaps you have a niggling sense that one of these life-changing moments is lurking around the corner waiting for you, but you just don't know what it is yet.

No matter where you stand right now on your path, I trust that since you're here, taking time to read this book, you believe in the power and possibility of turning point moments to help you create a better and more fulfilling life.

While the difficulties of the turning point experiences we face may not feel fabulous while we go through them, somewhere in the depths of your being, you know that good things can unfold as you navigate and grow through these impactful situations. The important thing—what you'll read about on these pages—is the resolve to know that what you're going through isn't something that's happening *to* you, it's something that is happening *for* you.

It doesn't matter if you're a leading-edge entrepreneur, schoolteacher, parent, rocket scientist, doctor, writer, healer, manager, salesperson, nurse, volunteer, retiree, or anything else; your life will bring you many of these pivotal moments. It's what you do with them and how you grow through them that makes all the difference.

These times we're living in are turning point moment times. You can't be alive on the planet right now and not be conscious in some way of the critical moments we are living in as a collective humanity. People ask: *What can I do? How can I make a difference?* One of the answers is to extract all the growth, healing, and transformation out of your personal turning point moments so you are a stronger, brighter, more resilient person who shines rays of hope and possibility for others in the world. We all need the reminder that we are strong enough to not only survive but thrive through these evolutionary times. Navigating these moments in our own lives is how we grow that resiliency.

In the pages of this book, you'll meet people who have grown through their turning point moments. My team and I feel blessed to have worked closely with the contributors to this book, coming together over the course of six months to birth this project for you. As you discover each contributor's story, you'll see why we consider it a privilege to call them our clients and comrades on the journey.

Some chapters may make you cry, while others may make you chuckle. Some will seem unbelievable or *out there*, while others may be touching reflections of your own turning point moment experience. Our hope is that every chapter offers you a heartfelt reassurance that if they can do *it*, you can too. If they can extract the good and use it to improve their lives, the same resiliency is available for you.

As you read through this book, I invite you to be lifted by what you read and to see some new possibilities for yourself and all people.

You don't need to read the chapters in order because as you peruse the table of contents or randomly flip open the pages, the chances are you will receive the exact message meant for you.

I also invite you to embrace the great diversity of the contributing authors. Their ethnicities, religious beliefs, career paths, backgrounds, and journeys are as diverse as can be. Yet, as you will see on the pages, their hearts all stand for the same thing—using their turning point moments as catalysts for positive change.

Above all else, let the stories in this book bathe you in possibility, hope, resolve, and inspiration to transform your turning point moment into beautiful blessings for yourself and others. On behalf of myself and all the contributing authors, we send you our deepest wish that these stories will deliver the inspiration you need as you create a life that works for you. May your life then cause a ripple effect of good in the world.

Blessings on your journey,

Christine Kloser
Founder and CEO, Get Your Book Done®
Founder and CEO, Capucia Publishing

CHAPTER 1

The Power of Persistence

Christine Kloser

I remember the day like it was yesterday. I was a new mother, with my three-month-old baby girl in my arms. It was May 2005, and I was standing in the sunshine, nursing her at a nondescript gas station somewhere about two hours west of Phoenix, Arizona. It was a monumental day for our new family. My husband, daughter, and I were on the first day of our road trip to move to Maryland after enjoying fourteen incredible years living in Los Angeles.

Once Janet was born, my maternal instinct kicked into full gear. We hadn't been planning to move, yet somewhere in our hearts, my husband and I never felt like Los Angeles would be our forever home. So, after Janet was born, we soon found ourselves subletting our apartment, telling friends we were going east for a few months to check it out, and packing up our belongings to venture back to the coast where I had been born and raised. Maternal instinct is a powerful thing.

We designed the trip to coincide with a family reunion my husband's family had planned in Park City, Utah. Actually, the reunion—and making the decision between flying there or driving there—was the impetus that tipped us over the edge to say, *Let's just drive and keep on driving.* So that's what we did. We planned a month-long adventure visiting family in Phoenix, Arizona and friends in Santa Fe, New Mexico, and exploring some of the beautiful parks and sights through Colorado and Utah. It was going to be amazing.

At least, I thought that until we got in the car to leave that nondescript gas station parking lot outside of Phoenix. Now, you may be thinking we must have been in a car crash or decided to turn around and not follow through with our spontaneous move to the East Coast. However, this turning point moment was not quite like that. It was something that seemed small and insignificant at first, but it changed the trajectory of my life from that day forward.

Let me paint the seemingly uneventful picture for you. Our 2002 Green Nissan Maxima was filled to the brim. The trunk was put together like a jig-saw puzzle in the way only my husband can pack a trunk. The back seat was packed with suitcases and the balance of what we needed to get us through our *three-month visit*, which we always knew was a permanent move. Janet was tucked into her car seat behind me, snug as a bug in a rug.

David was driving, and I was sitting in the tan leather passenger seat with my left hand gently resting on the shoulder of the driver's seat. It was a gorgeous day, and I was enjoying the view both out the window and over my left shoulder in the car seat behind me. She was such a beautiful baby. Eventually my arm got a little tired resting on the driver's seat, so I moved it to my lap.

Believe it or not, *that* was my turning point moment.

Something happened to my neck when I moved my arm off of the driver's seat, and the pain shot through my body like a hot, stabbing knife. *What the F*** was that?* I grabbed the left side of my neck immediately, as this was no ordinary neck twinge, and started rubbing it out, thinking that it was just some odd spasm that would go away in a few minutes.

We arrived at our family's house in Phoenix, and it still hurt badly. We got to New Mexico, where I found a chiropractor to treat me as soon as we arrived. The X-rays showed *nothing*, and after the treatment, it still hurt. We toured through Colorado and Utah, and the pain still stabbed and burned. In our photo album of that trip, there are very few photos of me holding Janet because it hurt too much for me to carry her, especially in her baby carrier. My neck kept hurting.

As soon as we arrived in Maryland, I found more doctors—and more X-rays showed nothing—yet I continued to be in serious, constant pain. It became so bad that I had my one and only panic attack as I made my husband put me in the car at 1:00 a.m. to drive me to the hospital. During the day, especially when I was home alone, it was equally as bad. I would sometimes just lie down on the ground and sob next to my daughter because she was crying, and I was in too much pain to pick her up out of fear of dropping her. Sometimes, the stabbing pain sent me to my knees.

I had maintained a great level of health and fitness prior to this debilitating move of my arm that day in the car. I grew up doing gymnastics, dancing, and competitive figure skating. I started teaching aerobics when I was eighteen and had a career in the fitness industry for twenty years. I was a personal trainer, fitness instructor, yoga teacher, and studio/gym owner before shifting to my career in the publishing industry. I continued to teach yoga right up until I gave birth. I was a healthy, fit woman. The operative word in that sentence is *was*.

My beautiful daughter turned seventeen earlier this year in 2022, and for all but the past year of her life, she's only known me to be in pain. It was a long, excruciating, and relentless journey to get to where I am today, but I can finally say that *was* is transforming to *is*. I feel my health, fitness, and pain-free life returning.

It took persistence, a level of persistence beyond what I knew was humanly possible. And faith. No matter how bad it got, including the day I reviewed my life insurance policy to see if David would still receive benefits if I ended my life, I never gave up. Something deep inside of me kept me going on a healing journey, trying nearly everything under the sun in pursuit of being free of the pain that debilitated me. I knew I was here for bigger and better things than being held back by chronic pain.

At last count, I've engaged in fifty different healing modalities: from traditional physical therapy, steroids, MD prescribed pain killers (including opioids it was so bad), neurological treatments, and surgical injections to the more holistic and natural modalities of acupuncture, neuro-modulation technique, psychedelics, homeopathy, functional medicine, shamanic healing, and dozens more.

The second big turning point in this healing journey was when I stepped away from my family and businesses for three weeks—thanks to my supportive husband and incredible business team—to go to John Barnes' *Therapy on the Rocks* in Sedona, Arizona. It was there that I experienced three intensive myo-fascial release treatments daily for eighteen days straight. While the treatments were painful, rigorous, and triggering at times, it was well worth every minute and dollar I spent. My body loved the work, responded well, and began to heal more deeply that it had in the previous sixteen years. Those weeks gave me hope for a better, pain-free future.

Had I not been relentlessly persistent in my pursuit of healing, I never would have landed in Sedona. I could have ended up addicted to prescription pain medication or miserable and buried under a rock of permanent defeat. But I didn't. I pursued. I persisted. I forged forward with my life and businesses, despite the pain. I forged forward in my healing, no matter how discouraging it felt at times. And boy, did it get difficult after years of modalities and lots of time and money spent to still hurt so much. The thing that saved me was the grit to keep going, and I'm not stopping now, even though I'm feeling better. As recently as the beginning of this year, I started Atlas-

Orthogonal chiropractic work and neurofeedback to continue feeling better and stronger every day.

Now, I'm dancing again nearly every day, and I'm able to enjoy better quality time with my family; be more present with my friends, team, and clients; focus more on my businesses; and even pursue starting a new endeavor. I also became certified to teach a fun dance fitness class called *Groove*®.

So when I tell you to be persistent through your own turning point moments and to never give up on the life you desire, I offer that encouragement from having spent seventeen years in the trenches on this journey myself. No matter what you're facing, no matter how uphill it may look sometimes, no matter the depth of the moments of defeat—you can do this! Keep believing in yourself, your growth, your healing, and the magnificent life that is seeking you just as much as you are seeking it. I believe in this better life for you, and I'm rooting for you every step of the way.

○

USA Today and *Wall Street Journal* best-selling author, **Christine Kloser** is the Founder and CEO of Get Your Book Done and Capucia Publishing. Since 2004, her companies have supported successful professionals and rising thought leaders through the powerful process of writing, publishing, and marketing their transformational books. She's impacted aspiring authors in 127 countries through her popular programs, including the *Book Breakthrough Quest*, the *Transformational Author Experience,* and the *Get Your Book Done* podcast. Get free help to start writing your book at: getyourbookdone.com/turningpoints

CHAPTER 2

Say Yes to You

Anela Arcari

A few years ago, I found myself sitting on the floor of my closet, earnestly praying and feverishly journaling. I had recently seen the movie *War Room*, which I assumed was a military movie based on the title. Much to my surprise, it was an inspirational movie about praying and journaling (and much more), and it inspired me to set up a *war room* in my closet like the one depicted in the movie.

At that time, I was in a romantic relationship that I knew in my heart was over, and I struggled to end it. I felt hopeless and desperate to feel happy. In that low point, I wrote in my journal: *There has to be a better way to live life*. I was clear that I did not like my life in that moment. That's how I found myself on the floor, pleading for help because I knew I had to do something, anything different to have a better result. I knew I could not continue to do the same thing and expect a healthier, more fulfilling life. Looking back, I realize I was looking outside of myself for my joy and happiness.

The very next day, I miraculously received an email with the subject line: *Are you looking for a miracle?*

I thought to myself, *Yes, I am!* The email was sent by a woman I first met during the Pennsylvania Governor's annual women's conference twelve years earlier. After listening to her presentation about living the life of your dreams, I signed up for her weekly emails. As often happens, I seldom, if ever, read them. Instead, I placed them in a folder labeled *Dreams* and told myself that one day I would go back and read them. Yet, on this day, twelve years later, the word *miracle* in the subject line drew me in. I opened her email, curious about how to find a miracle.

The email provided a link to sign up for a free call to learn about a program, "Your Year of Miracles." Without even thinking about it, I found myself signing up for the call, putting it on my calendar, and anxiously awaiting the additional information. A few days later, I joined the call and fell in love with the energy and enthusiasm of the co-founders, Marci Shimoff and Debra Poneman. This was before video conferencing, so all I heard were their voices on a telephone. During the call, they offered a yearlong program, a personal transformation course to help create the conditions for miracles to happen. Given how hopeless and dejected I had felt the night before, I noticed myself signing up for the program before the end of the call. I remember feeling as if a huge weight was lifted off my shoulders as soon as I said yes to the course.

What inspired me to say yes? One of the co-founders explained why she felt called to offer a yearlong personal growth journey. At this point, she read this traditional Chinese proverb:

> If there is light in the soul, there will be beauty in the person. If there is beauty in the person, there will be harmony in the house. If there is harmony in the house, there will be order in the nation. If there is order in the nation, there will be peace in the world.

Upon hearing this beautiful, succinct maxim, I was all in. While I had heard many times before that peace or love or whatever you seek begins with the person staring back at you in the mirror, I never really understood it until I heard this proverb. I had never felt a tingling sensation in my entire body the way I did that day when I heard these profound statements.

That was the day I said yes to me—the day I looked in the mirror, knowing that world peace started with me. I was finishing up a twenty-eight-year career in the military in which I felt I made a difference preserving peace and freedom. Much of that felt external to me, going where I was most needed. I loved every minute of my calling to serve in the military, but I was now in the position to spend more time with the woman looking at me in the mirror.

I enthusiastically made the yearlong commitment to grow beyond my comfort zone, to learn about living more consciously, to move forward, and to raise my vibration every single day. After participating in the first call, I increased my membership to the highest level, which included twenty one-on-one sessions with a life coach. Up until this point, I considered myself a lifelong seeker, and I had not ever consistently practiced anything I had learned. The Chinese proverb resonated so strongly with me that I jumped in with both feet and began steadily, day by day, to take active steps towards uncovering the light in my soul.

You may have heard that until the pain becomes so great you can't live with it anymore, you won't be motivated to act. For me, sitting on the floor in my closet, crying and pleading for a better way was my pain point. Asking for help, receiving the email, opening and reading the email, and deciding to take the next step was a life-altering turning point for me. Had I listened to the call and not taken any action, would I be where I am today? Maybe, I don't know. What I do know is so much began to unfold from the moment I said yes to me.

Retiring from the Army after growing up in a military family and serving my country for twenty-eight years was a significant emotional event. The bi-monthly coaching sessions helped me tremendously as I navigated my considerable grief. As confident as I was standing in front of a formation of four hundred or more soldiers, I was not always as confident when standing up for myself.

During the pandemic, I began to step out of my comfort zone when I joined a writing group that provided invaluable feedback on my short stories. I then stepped further out of my comfort zone when I was asked to be an executive producer on a documentary that tells the story of a woman who survived the Boston marathon bombings and chose to heal herself naturally. I knew nothing about making a film or even the executive producer's role. These events and so many more unfolded when I said yes to me.

I don't want to give the impression that this personal growth path is easy. I was told early on that creating the conditions for miracles is simple and not always easy. I found that it takes consistent commitment every day. Five years later, I am still an active member of "Your Year of Miracles," working with an amazing life coach, Leila, becoming all I can be, knowing this is a lifelong journey. From the first year, I knew I was here to write and coach; I just didn't know what to write or how to coach or share my words. I still don't and being a part of this book is my way of saying yes to me again. In fact, the opportunity to write this chapter came from the yes to "Your Year of Miracles."

During my first year in the miracles program, I met a woman who introduced me to Christine Kloser three years later. Taking this step to write a chapter in an inspirational book is yet another step onto a bigger stage. Looking at the proverb, I now understand I shine the light in my soul through written words and coaching. I now know there is beauty in me, and I have *harmony in my house* because I bought my first house last year. According to that Chinese proverb, I am now up to *order in the nation*, which is only one step away from *peace in the world*.

You may read this and think it is a tall order—maybe it is. It starts with finding the light in your soul and creating a life that works for you.

If you want to a create a life that works for you, I have some suggestions:

1. *Say Yes to You*—this may require stepping out of your comfort zone which can lead to personal growth.
2. Find support through a course or a coach.
3. Shine, shine, shine the light in your soul.

Only when we look back can we connect the dots that have brought us to our own light, to our destiny. In my experience, the path to and from my turning point led to personal inner growth and made all the difference. May this chapter and book inspire you to say yes to you, become all you can be, and create a life that works for you.

Anela Arcari is a combat engineer veteran with twenty-eight years of service turned intuitive, mystical counselor. An executive producer and aspiring author, Anela's innate gifts elicit the best transformation for her clients. She is a highly recommended and sought-after leadership and personal growth coach, speaker, and mentor. Anela holds a MS in Education (Leadership Development and Counseling) and is a National Certified Counselor (NCC). Connect with Anela at linkedin.com/in/anelaarcari

CHAPTER 3

Stepping Out

Lyla Berg

My turning point moment started with her words, "You're probably going to hate me for the rest of your life, but I have to tell you—your husband is having an affair with _____."

So began my interaction with the governor's wife at a New Year's Eve party—and the beginning of a life I would never have imagined for myself.

Later that night when we got home from the party, I asked my husband what the governor's wife was talking about. His answer was, "She (the other woman) is going to leave our city until this noise blows over." He then rolled over in bed and went to sleep.

The next morning, I told him we evidently needed to fix our relationship and that he had to find somewhere else to live unless he was willing to do three things: take an HIV blood test, attend marital counseling with me, and sign back to me the properties and assets I had provided from my family trust. I was holding our one-year-old baby when I told him that he had one week to decide whether to stay married to me and agree to the three conditions, or leave forever, with or without the other woman.

He departed the house that morning with no comment. In the midst of my anguish, I made the decision to rise above. I had the door locks changed, cancelled the credit cards, withdrew money from all the accounts, and called my mother-in-law to explain what happened. As the end of the week approached with no communication from him, I put his clothes neatly, deliberately, and systematically in large black garbage bags. When the last day of the week came, I placed the bags in the middle of our cul-de-sac and called his office manager to pick up the items before the garbage truck arrived in the morning.

For months, I suspected that my husband was having an affair, but I didn't want to confront him for fear of his retribution. I had already experienced too many occasions where physical, mental, and emotional abuse were his reactions to a question I asked, a remark I made, or an inadvertent action I did. My intuition was correct. His lack of intention to stay with me and work through our relationship was obvious. Divorcing him was my only option to keep my sanity and protect myself and my one-year-old child.

Up until that moment, I thought courage was what heroes and heroines showed in the fight between good and evil. With a Filipino-Chinese mother and a German-Dutch father twenty years older than my mom, I grew up as an obedient, self-disciplined, and accommodating person who followed the rules and did what she was told. I was raised to be a *lady*, and according to my mother, *Ladies don't get angry, raise their voices, express distress, or show any reaction other than control.* I believed that being a supportive, loving wife meant subjugating my feelings, opinions, and desires in deference to my husband. Keeping peace in the household was my ultimate goal and responsibility.

My then-husband was a teacher when we married and quickly became a person of political influence in elected, local government within two years of our wedding. For years after our marriage ended, I focused on what I had lost in court because of the pressure he exerted over the judge during the divorce proceedings. By court order, I was instructed to give him three properties, my horses, and the balance of the trust account my father established for me upon his death. I was not awarded alimony, and the court directed me to pay him child support, even though the baby was residing with me full-time, and I was responsible for all my son's medical, educational, and living expenses. Most significantly, however, I lost my self-esteem and sense of personal power.

Critical moments in our lives cause us to question who we are. However, sometimes one never knows what a situation really means until much later. Looking back, I now realize how much I gained. Who would have anticipated that the concerned words of the governor's wife would be the catalyst for me to discover my own courage? Who could have guessed that my gratitude for her honesty would help me develop compassion for myself and regain self-respect? By getting divorced, I stepped out of a debilitating situation and into a lifelong commitment to assist women and children in building their self-esteem. Instead of seeing myself as a victim, I *tightened my belt*, trusted my inner voice, and put one foot in front of the other to keep myself emotionally upright. Subsequently, my newly-revealed internal strength led me to explore, discover, and ultimately turn what happened into an asset-building life trajectory.

As a career educator, my personal philosophy was: *When the going gets tough, the tough go back to school*—a place I knew I could be successful. I consequently embarked on a PhD program focusing on self-esteem. I needed to understand the choices in relationships I had made throughout my life. A requirement of the program was to undertake a personal growth project centered on my passions, rather than scholarly research. I started formal voice instruction, began taking acting lessons, and enrolled in dance classes. I was encouraged to audition for community theater performances and landed several leading roles in various local venues. I even signed up with a casting agency to audition for TV commercials, which ultimately prepared me to be the host of local talk-show television programs. I am filled with gratitude for everyone who encouraged me to try different activities as I was healing from the divorce experience.

Upon receiving my doctorate, I decided to leave my full-time, seventeen-year public school career to teach in the College of Education at our local university. I firmly believed that if teachers understood the critical role self-esteem plays in developing personal strength and character, they would be more deliberate in designing learning opportunities for youth. Ultimately, I established my own training company for leadership development to support the self-esteem of adults in the work force, knowing that they would influence the young people with whom they were connected. I even started a non-profit educational voting program for youth with the slogan, *Our Voices DO Count,* so young people would know they are valued and *heard.*

It takes courage to get divorced because divorce is not a final action, but rather, a starting point. Choosing to leave a relationship is a step in the doorway that opens into The Unknown. That can be terrifying, or exhilarating, depending upon one's personal stamina. It takes courage to quit a job, raise a child as a single parent, recover from financial loss, and believe in love again. It takes courage to wake up and know you have to face each day, alone. It took courage and self-trust for me to assert what I believed was right, even though, on some days, the pain was almost unbearable. Now I *know,* however, that each one of us is capable of rising above anything that life throws our way.

Some people believe that holding on—whether to a person, relationship, job, emotion, or belief—is a sign of strength. I learned that it takes much more strength to know when to let go and then to do it. Letting go doesn't mean you don't care about someone or something anymore. It's simply realizing that your well-being matters and that you can truly only influence your own actions. Sometimes, there are things or people in our lives that are just not meant to stay.

It's the changes we don't want that actually become the springboards for us to grow. Growth and change can be painful, but nothing in life is as agonizing as staying stuck where you know you don't belong.

I had a professional career, a house mortgage, and a baby when I chose to get divorced. I trusted that a better future waited for me beyond the heartbreak of betrayal, domestic abuse, and anxiety about financially supporting myself and my son. It is important to pause and reflect occasionally, and with gratitude, on specific incidents or periods of time in our lives that pushed us into uncharted territory. All decisions affect our life journey. However, some choices catapult us on paths of such heights and unprecedented speed that it is only in reflection that we can fully appreciate the significance of what occurred and how far we have come as a result.

During the entire two-year divorce process, my father's words while I was growing up accompanied my nightly prayers and became my daily mantra: *Per aspera ad astra—through hardships to the stars.* Those words helped me rise above my fears, disappointments, and self-doubt. My personal transformation occurred slowly as I made peace with myself for my past choices and allowed myself to simply be enough. In gratitude for everyone and everything that occurs in my life, I now choose to believe that we are here for a Divine purpose, perhaps as yet to be fully revealed.

You, too, may be simply trying to put one foot in front of the other—to find your way through a dark moment. Having courage to step out of what is familiar or expected is your only option if you want to live true to yourself. You *can* do it!

Lyla Berg is an international educator, professional speaker, and resiliency coach. She is the owner and principal consultant with Lyla Berg & Associates, a training organization devoted to assisting companies and individuals to develop values-driven leadership, collaborative relationships, and effective communication skills. Lyla is an accomplished theater actress and Argentine tango dancer. She also hosts her own public television program in Hawai‘i. Lyla can help you step out and live life on *your* terms! Please visit: LeavingTheGildedCage.com

CHAPTER 4

Walking in Faith

Christine Bernard

In 2016, I inherited my granddaughter Keegan. Keegan, then four years old, was born at thirty weeks gestation and had a brain bleed that left her muscles stiff. She was unable to walk without assistance and was eventually diagnosed with cerebral palsy (CP). I say I inherited Keegan because my daughter-in-law decided to leave my son—and the state. Keegan was left behind, and my son asked me to take her.

Having Keegan's mother leave was a blessing since she was doing very little to help Keegan's progress. My daughter-in law would take no advice or help. I found out that caring for special needs kids is a full-time job. Although I am a registered nurse, I knew very little about CP as my background is in critical care, and I felt like a detective attempting to find any information on what kind of assistance there was for special needs kids. Through Keegan's pre-school, I found out about the Office for People with Developmental Disabilities (OPWDD). Programs like OPWDD are available in every state under different names.

I had no idea of the amount of time and effort it took caring for a special needs child and was more than a little overwhelmed. My son was of little help; because of his own issues, he could hardly take care of himself.

Most of my resources for helping Keegan came from caregivers of other special needs children and physical therapists. To date we have done multiple off-label therapies to improve Keegan's mobility. There is no magic pill for kids with CP, but I saw improvement in Keegan's fine motor skills, especially handwriting and in using her right arm—which she wasn't doing before these treatments—and in her walking.

When the COVID pandemic hit in March of 2020, I was working in a procedural center, having left the hospital three years prior. Everyone working in our center was told we would be going to the hospital to help with the influx of COVID patients as our elective procedures were on hold. It was a scary time for our world since so little was known about this virus. From a television at work one day, I heard our Governor say, "This is a virus 90 percent of us can get and not even know we have." *Okay, I can do this.*

Nothing could have prepared me for what I saw in the hospital. It looked like a war zone. As fearful as I was to care for COVID patients, I am grateful to have had this experience. The staffing was minimal until the traveling nurses came, and the comradery of the hospital workers was so amazing. No one complained, and we were all on board.

I cried going to work every day, seeing the empty roads and shutdown stores. Every night on the way home, I cried for all the suffering I witnessed. Most patients were on ventilators and multiple intravenous (IV) drips—for sedation, pain, to keep their blood pressure up—and many were on a paralytic agent so they could not move. Any muscle movement uses oxygen, so if keeping a patient's oxygen saturation up was critical, the patient was paralyzed to conserve oxygen. Can you imagine lying in a bed and not being able to interact with your environment at all, or anyone who came into the room, all the while being able to hear everything that is said? It was heartbreaking, and I still get emotional talking about it.

At home, I was banished to my finished basement for fear of bringing the virus home to my family. My two grandsons also lived with us, ages twelve and fourteen, and my heart went out to them for being robbed of a normal life. My son and his girlfriend took over Keegan's care, and I had a lot more time on my hands. I prayed a lot for this virus to go away and about all the chaos in the world. The censorship, the constantly changing narrative, the loss of our freedoms, and the overreach in control of medicine were all things that concerned me, and I used my time to research and learn as much as I could about what was happening in our world and the virus. This type of world was not what I wanted my grandchildren to inherit.

I went back to meditating and doing yoga. Being blessed with good friends is what helped me most during the early days of the pandemic. Weekly Zoom meetings, bike rides in the cold to the water for a picnic on the beach, and driveway birthday celebrations all gave me comfort and basically kept me from losing my mind. I was so worried and fearful of everything that was happening.

By June, we were back in our procedural center at work as the height of the pandemic was winding down at the hospital. I went back to caring for Keegan and working five days a week instead of the three days, twelve-and-a-half-hour work week. Schools were closed, and I learned how difficult it was to home school special needs kids and to keep track of my two grandsons' schoolwork. I was grateful to the college students who were with Keegan during the day, but I couldn't always get them, and on those days, I was helping her with schoolwork. Besides the regular subjects, the school also wanted them to do art, music, gym, library, and Keegan's physical and occupational therapy, virtually. This was impossible. One person could not take care of her physical needs, cook for her, and take on all the roles the school wanted. Just doing the main school subjects kept Keegan at the kitchen table most of the day.

I was not coping well with all the extra work in the house. Between feeling overworked at home and fearful of what was happening in the world, it was hard for me to function. My behavior became critical—complaining and controlling—to the point that when I entered a room, everyone would scatter. Everyone except Keegan, of course. I did not like the person I was.

I started praying for guidance, and besides my church, found some good on-line preachers who helped keep me centered. I realized that although I was a believer, I was more of an admirer of Jesus and had not actually accepted him as my Lord and Savior. I worked on opening my heart and listening to what I was told to do, which led me to becoming more compassionate, loving, and kind and less controlling and judgmental. I watched my life improve, and I lost my fear.

We now live in a world that we would not have believed possible two years ago. If we all settle for being optimistic, feeling this is all going away on its own, it will not. It would be like me being optimistic about Keegan ever becoming an independent walker and then doing nothing to help her achieve that goal. All of us must do our part in moving our lives, families, communities, and our world into a better place.

We must all do whatever we can whenever we see something we don't like. No matter how small an action is by one person, collectively our actions can amount to a lot. Whether we say a prayer, send a letter, email our legislature, join a rally, improve a situation at work, or just strive to be more loving and kind, our actions will help improve our world. No action is too small, and we cannot judge the actions of others or their choices. It is time for all of us to accept our differences and come together. If we can keep our eyes on how we want the story to end, while accepting our present reality, it can prompt us to act.

Keegan is now ten years old and still cannot pull herself to stand, sit up without assistance, climb in a chair, or dress herself. The other day, I looked at Keegan; she had her lip pouted out, and there were tears running down her face.

I knew Keegan was having her occasional pity party, and I told her it was okay.

"Why me?" Keegan asked. "I just want to walk."

I told Keegan I didn't know the answer to her question. I held her and told her to cry until there was nothing left, and I cried with her. When Keegan was done crying, I asked her if she knew a joke because we both needed one, and that made her laugh. Healing Keegan and healing our world may seem impossible and may take a miracle, but God specializes in miracles. There is nothing more supernatural than Jesus being raised from the dead. As I walk my path, I will keep doing and believing, knowing that I do not walk alone.

In dealing with life situations that seem insurmountable, I have learned that starting my day with gratitude and prayer is foremost. Keeping in the present moment of what is needed today, letting go of outcomes to problems while taking the steps I am guided to do, is the only thing that has given me peace.

How do you want your story to end? Keep focused on that, be the best you can be today, and replace worry and fear with positive thoughts of the future. Need a miracle? They are real, but only if you believe.

○

Christine Bernard is a retired registered nurse of thirty-six years. She worked in critical care for most of her career and was certified in critical care for over twenty years. At the height of the COVID pandemic, she worked for three months with corona virus patients. Christine is also a certified yoga instructor and Reiki Master. She has a bachelor's degree in science with a major in nursing.

CHAPTER 5

Leaping Beyond the Known

Kathryn Brewer

The screaming in my ears was blocking out all the words I knew were directed at me. What did I miss? How was I to respond?

My tinnitus was at its worst that day. It had been building. I was discouraged and yes, angry. I had done the *impossible* in healing twenty-five years of undiagnosed Lyme Disease through alternative energy healing and a year of sometimes excruciating pain. That year of effort was supposed to cure the tinnitus. It didn't. It did relieve a host of other physical limitations and was worth that horrendous and beautiful year, but I was left with *what now*?

I fell into what I called a *mini dark night of the soul*. I wanted to leave this too-hard life and go home to the dimensions of love that I never ceased knowing due to the near-death experience I had during my birth. As always, I came to some peace from remembering I was called to Earth and had a purpose here that was, as yet, unclear. I would somehow find the way again.

Have you ever felt that on the outside you appear to have a quite satisfactory, even successful life, yet you know there is more? You might even sense an inner magnet pulling you toward a dramatically expanded version of yourself. In these transformative times, that magnet has geometrically intensified. How do you find the direction, the steps, the courage to change your life structure and liberate your future self?

I had practiced confronting myself and hidden *idols* of belief and habits for decades, ever since I dredged up the courage to get divorced in a family that considered divorce sinful and a failure. I knew how to hold my feet to the fire when I wanted to run away if I knew the path. Yet, I was out of clues about how to heal the debilitating screaming in my ears.

The Universe/Source/God always comes through. So, the Universe stepped up while I was at a retreat, and that screaming tinnitus hijacked an important conversation at lunch. I explained why I didn't hear what she said, and the wise shaman said, "There is a message wanting to come through that you are denying."

Boom. The clue.

What clues are you receiving that either go unnoticed or are a mystery as to their meaning and application? In my course, *Language of the Universe*, I list fourteen *dialects,* such as numbers, oracles, sacred geometry, dreams, animals, books, Divine Appointments, and others. In this case, my clues were a conversation and a Divine Appointment.

The clues went on. The shaman told me about a past life in Egypt when important cosmic information intended for me was seized by another and the transmission was halted. That information was now needed on the planet.

Coming from a conservatively religious tiny town in the middle of the midwestern plains had inculcated me with fear of anything outside of the dogma, and I had only recently embraced reincarnation and my unbidden connection to the Akashic Records. Now my whole body responded with floods of energy, and I could not dismiss her information. I sensed the Egypt experience across time and space.

Perhaps like you, my childhood taught me to be on constant alert, so I could be one step ahead of danger and pain. I played an outer game of obedience while inside I trusted no one, not even my own heart. And now, I was being asked to trust what I could not see. How could I trust my worthiness to receive something important to humanity? *Note:* Worthiness has nothing to do with your soul's choice of your path/destiny.

The choice I made in the next moment changed my life. I agreed to allow the information to come through me. The frequent mini dark nights of the soul stopped. I began to feel that Earth could be more like home. I found a substitute for the old unsupported rules and beliefs I clung to for order in my life. I set weekly appointments to *meet* with the cosmic holders of the ancient information.

That choice was so foreign to whom I believed I was. I was a professional, based in science. I was grounded and reliable and practical, I thought. I was not the *woo woo* space cadet. None of those perceptions lent themselves easily to being a channel. I have since redefined channeling to put it in its rightful place as a normal aspect of life on Earth. Then, it was like saying I was a charlatan fortune teller, shrouded in dark and mist.

How do you respond when your cherished beliefs and ways of perceiving the world are challenged? These are times of a huge increase in the light on the planet, causing the dismantling of old unsustainable systems. In this chaos, how do we now find our clues?

This choice turned my self-identity upside down and created the portal to the spiritual transcendent experience that burst my heart open to Universal Love. What choices are you facing that feel like they could have a similar disruptive effect? What choices are you avoiding for that reason?

You might ask yourself, *Who do I believe I am?* Are you a teacher, a free-spirit, a nurturer, a stable provider, a credible professional, a hard-worker, a spiritual leader, the one with answers, or the one who holds the family together? While these may be some of your characteristics or roles, how does believing this is who you are limit your possibilities? You are so much more.

If you'd like to explore going beyond the boxes of your self-belief, take a few moments to breathe slowly in and out of your heart. Request that sacred space and divine protection encompass you. Imagine, sense, feel, see yourself as pure soul, timeless, before your birth. Ask, *What did I come here to be* (not do)? *What primary lessons did I choose? What message did I come to bring?* You might want to journal these questions or consult a Language of the Universe.

The answers to these questions can form meta-intentions for your life. For example, one of mine is: *I intend to fully experience every morsel of every life experience.* That intention helps me lean into situations that I would otherwise resist and receive greatly expanded gifts from those situations. Sending your meta-intentions consciously into the Quantum Field magnifies their beneficial co-orchestration of your life.

My life now is orchestrated by the Multiverse. More grounded and present on Earth than ever before, I start every day in communication with the highest vibrational energy/consciousnesses aligned with that day. They are not my gurus. We co-create in harmony with Source, Divine Intelligence, the Quantum Field. We are all aspects of that and co-travelers back to the Oneness from which we came.

Your journey may be quite different from mine. Yet, my observation of my life—and many clients who come to me to release what holds them back from being all they feel they have come to be—reveals a pattern. We are being called to stretch, to muster the courage to leap beyond our known, to trust the always loving and supportive intent of the Universe, and to step across the threshold into our future self. And in doing so, we affect and inspire whole segments of humanity toward the same.

You don't do this alone. We are being magically connected with other souls who are to walk the journey beside us. You may need to venture into places or online groups that are outside your typical choices. You may simply intend that you find your soul tribe and stay present to whomever enters your life.

If you are reading this book, you are likely part of the cadre of souls who have chosen to have a part in leading humanity during these times the ancients called *no time*. What follows is from my perceptive filters and the cosmic guides to which I relate. Please take in only what resonates with you.

Your part may be as a visible harbinger of change and inspiration or as a holder of the energy of love and Oneness that influences whomever you touch. Your part may flow in a gently expanding river through life, or you may have chosen to experience pain, darkness, and oppression in order to release and transmute that energy for the benefit of humankind. Whatever your choice, you are being called now to step up.

The light, vibrational codes, and energy matrices now on the planet have never been present before. Those of you who have buried memories of persecution in the past from shining your light are now safe. Yes, discernment is important. Ask to whom and when you should share what you know; sharing the energy of who you are is always beneficial. Together we can tip the balance toward recognition of our Oneness with one another and with Source. It is time for our future selves.

Time Is Now

The time is NOW—No messin' around!
Release the bonds with which we've been bound.

Our souls cry out to taste the promise
Of life that's free of *shame upon us.*

The journey has been long and intense
To prepare for our expanded sense

Of the wondrous design now in view,
Bringing new order to what's askew.

Lifting the fog so we clearly see—
We can say *YES* to our destiny.

Kathryn Brewer utilizes her personal transformation from Psychotherapist and School Psychologist to Transformational Mentor, Author, Speaker, and Certified Agent of Conscious Evolution Guide to create programs and Essence Alignment sessions that catapult her clients' satisfaction, impact, and expression of purpose to greater heights. Her life-long multidimensional connection infuses love into her Mentors of the Future Community, bringing together evolutionary souls to share higher wisdom and influence self and humanity toward oneness and joy. Contact her at: kathryn@kathrynbrewer.com

CHAPTER 6

This Is Me!

Leslie Bridger

I lay in bed, unable to move as tears streamed down my face. Even though the sun was shining through my window, across my bedspread, and onto the wall, I felt completely immersed in darkness. I started to sob uncontrollably and couldn't stop. As my chest heaved in and out with all the pain and heaviness I was feeling, I thought I'd suffocate.

I was living the *American Dream*, wasn't I? I looked extremely successful on the outside, yet felt a deep emptiness and sadness on the inside. I had everything I thought would make me happy—a successful career, a wonderful and loving life partner, a beautiful home, a lot of money and so much more—yet I was miserable.

What is wrong with me? How did I get to this place? What have I done wrong? These questions, along with a never-ending tirade of shame and blame, kept running through my mind nonstop. I didn't have the strength to fight these emotions and my feelings of unhappiness any longer. It was as if the dam I had erected many moons ago had broken, and everything I had pushed down in the past kept flooding to the surface.

Just when I thought my tears were subsiding, they'd start pouring out once again. As this pattern continued for what seemed like eons, I envisioned a newspaper article with the title "Woman Drowns in Her Own Tears." That could be a possibility, I thought, as my cheek rested on my soaked pillowcase.

Something else was unfolding as I allowed myself to feel everything I had been afraid to feel for over twenty years. The businesswoman I was thought it odd that in the midst of my breakdown, I actually started to feel lighter. It's as if, at the end of a long tunnel of darkness, I could see a faint glimmer of light, a tiny spark of hope that was beckoning me to rise up. It all started to make sense as my raining tears cleared the heavy, dense energy I had become encased in. These feelings had been bubbling to the surface for a number of years as I climbed the corporate ladder.

During that climb, my food addiction, which started when the sexual abuse began at age eleven, kicked in big time. Whenever any thought or feeling I didn't want to acknowledge or experience would rear its ugly head, I ate. It didn't matter what time of the day or night it was or where I was, I used food to fill the void I felt within. I felt like a zombie with no control. I wanted—and part of me thought I truly needed—anything to distract me from the uneasiness I was feeling: chips, chocolate, cookies, ice cream, greasy fried food, or any other grub I could find in my freezer, fridge, cupboard, or office drawer. As I mindlessly ate whatever was in front of me, the food would temporarily numb me. With each rung on the so-called ladder of success I climbed, the feelings intensified.

Depleted from shedding a river of tears, I could feel the heaviness of my body against my mattress. It took every ounce of strength I had to crawl out of bed. I felt such shame and embarrassment as I looked at my pale face and overweight, unhealthy, and unfit body in the mirror. I didn't know the woman who timidly looked at me with no life in her gaze and wondered, *How the hell did I get here?*

Then, there was an energy shift. I couldn't explain at the time why I suddenly felt immense love flushing through my body as I peered at the empty shell of a woman I saw before me. I now know it was my soul, the highest version of myself, wrapping me in her loving energy. She understood this was the breakdown I needed to break through to a happier, healthier me in all areas of my life. *When was I last happy?* I asked myself. Instantly, I traveled back to my teenage years.

I saw that version of me through a new, kind, and loving lens. She had a powerful self-care practice that had kept her strong and empowered in the daily challenges she was experiencing. I saw her escaping to her favourite places in nature, her camera strap slung over her shoulder when the pain within her was so strong she could barely breathe. The memories came flooding back to me. As soon as she stepped foot on Mother Earth's sacred ground, she felt embraced and supported like never before. Whenever she did that, which was almost daily, everything seemed to open up before her. Where before all she could see was her own pain and misery, she now saw the beauty and wonder in the simple things of life.

As she was capturing the incredible moments of awe and wonder that nature gifts us every single day in the photographs she felt guided to create, she was whisked into another world—one where miracles, hope, and possibilities were the norm. Mother Earth, along with her camera and latest journal, had been her constant companions for years. She always felt better about herself and life whenever they were together. *How did she travel from there to where I am now?*

I saw myself in the mid-70s, around fifteen or sixteen, standing in front of my parents. I knew how nature and the images I created in those sacred spaces were healing—not only for me but also for others. I bared my heart and soul to them as I shared my dreams of being a photographer full-time. I excitedly told them about my vision. Quickly, my bubble was burst by my loving, caring, and well-meaning parents, a physician and college instructor. They exchanged worried glances with each other before they said, "You'll never make money as a photographer. You need to go to university, earn a degree, so you can get a real job. You can take photographs as a hobby, Honey." I felt small, deflated, and sick to my stomach as I realized that what I wanted wasn't important or valued. My path of pushing down what made me come alive and doing instead what I could to fit in and be like everyone else began on that day.

Another picture flashed across my mind, one of cattle being rounded up in a cage of sameness and mediocrity. After living the life I was told I should be living for over twenty years, it's no wonder I felt dead inside. I had forgotten who I truly was and what brought me joy. My beloved camera was lost at the bottom of my storage closet and hadn't been used in years. As I thought of dusting off my camera and going outside in nature, I could feel myself coming alive.

From that moment on, I did what I could to remember and reclaim my authentic self, that young girl who was happy and hopeful in the midst of the challenges she was facing. Day by day, week by week, month by month, and year by year, I became a sculptor chipping away at the stone walls she had erected around her heart and soul that had been hurt all those years ago.

***

Now, twenty years have passed, and here I am, no longer barely existing in my life. Every challenge I have been through since that tear-filled day have all been opportunities for me to grow and evolve. To name a few:

- My mom was diagnosed with terminal cancer and given months to live.
- My life-partner and I split after almost eighteen years together.
- I almost lost my life from a traumatic brain injury I received in a bicycle accident.

Through it all, my camera, latest journal, and Mother Earth have been my best friends and constant companions. I am alive and thriving, absolutely loving myself and my life because of them.

So, dear reader, I'm sure you have, or someone you know has, experienced what I'm talking about. There are millions around the globe who have become someone they're not to please others or to fit in with what society expects. I'm certainly not alone. If you don't feel you're aligned with the highest version of yourself, living a life you absolutely love, then this could be you. If it is, it's time to listen to that voice within that has been screaming out to be seen and heard. Ask the places within you that feel shut down or shut off to speak. Capture the *Aha!*s and insights you receive in whatever way works best for you. This could be through audio, video, journaling with a pen and paper, or typing your answers on your laptop.

What does your authentic self want you to remember and reclaim? What's one small step you can take today—not tomorrow, next week, or next month—to start loving, embracing, and honouring who you really are?

As I write this, I just listened to my new favourite song, "This Is Me," *The Greatest Showman*'s theme song. It has become my new anthem. I refuse to dim my light anymore! I am here, proudly and unapologetically standing in my truth, fully embracing who I am and my unique gifts, skills, and talents. I am here to share with the world to make it a better place, and I encourage you to do the same. The world definitely needs our bright lights.

$\bigcirc$

Leslie Bridger's turning point came when the never-ending supply of junk food she used to mindlessly stuff in her face didn't numb her emptiness anymore. Her upcoming book, *Alive and Thriving: Miraculous Healing Above and Beyond the Odds*, is the one she wished she had when she was struggling emotionally to find meaning in life again and physically healing after a near-fatal bicycle accident. Please visit lesliebridger.com to receive her complimentary guided meditation, "Remember Who You Are."

CHAPTER 7

Sound of Sharon

Sharon M. Carrington

Familiar Sounds

Music and sounds are synonymous with my life. I love music! The healing properties are myriad. It can change my feelings to being happy, sad, reflective, or can dissipate all negative feelings in an instant. I refer to music as healing in my life and one of many tools that can help me or anyone get through any situation.

Have you had or experienced a situation in your life that you didn't know how to get through? Come along with me on my recent adventure, and see if I can be of help to you.

At the beginning of the pandemic, I was working in a corporation that was resizing from a recent purchase. At any time, we were due to move into the new building and go from our small ten-person department to hundreds of people on a floor. Everyone was a bit nervous but looking forward to seeing how everything would work out. The night before St. Patrick's Day in 2020, one of our staff members' spouses had been exposed to someone with COVID-19. I knew something was wrong as I drove up to the parking lot and it was practically empty. Upon arrival, I was set up to work remotely from home with all needed equipment as I was considered to be in the higher risk category. I hadn't been nervous up to that point, but I felt dread creeping over me as I was waiting for everything to get set up. After being there six hours, I was finally set up with everything needed to work from home and happily went home to set up my new workspace.

Our corporate move was put on hold indefinitely, and we all navigated our new work environments. I loved being able to have my sliding glass door open to hear the birds sing, to listen to the squirrels playing, and to take my breaks walking around the neighborhood observing all the newness around me that I now had time to truly see. My doldrum job took on new life in this new environment and the sights and sounds that went with it. Every day, we had a meeting at 3 p.m. to see each other and communicate, so we didn't feel cut off from the outside world. We could show our face or not; that was our choice. I was thriving in this new foreign world of COVID-19.

No Sounds

Alas, on January 20, 2021, everything changed. My manager called and said I was one of many who were being downsized by the new company. My last workday would be Feb. 18—no insurance after the end of February, no pay for vacation time over forty hours (I had just accrued quite a bit more as of the new year), and I would receive four weeks of severance pay. Job search help with the company would be provided. *Any questions?*

I faded out entirely as the phone call ended, totally numb as that familiar spiral and fog of depression started spinning around me. I thought I was ready for this day, but the tears streamed down my face as I laid my head down on my worktable. I wanted to curl up into a ball in my bed and stay. The next few days were a blur. I had no appetite, no desire to fill out forms online to be contacted by the Human Resources job search team for job search help and assistance. I did listen to the one ninety-minute call so all of us could be aware of what to expect going forward. My environment that had been so lively and full of sound and color was now monotone and drab. All I could hear from the HR personnel was sadness and pity. Many of the questions we had could only be answered with a phone number. This number was for customer service who could not answer anything either.

What was I to expect? I had given away my power, connected my self-worth to a job, a title, a nine-to-five. Didn't Dolly Parton write a song about this years ago of the dangers of "Working 9 to 5?" Just the thought of this song gave me a little bit of a smile.

Ah! Okay, this is a start. Now to begin my healing journey.

Healing Sounds

I knew I needed to put myself on a schedule to do everything I could think of to be good to myself and see myself as a real person again. I was far from it at this point. I still had my beautiful outdoors, my wonderful plants and animals, and more time to walk outside. I started getting up early to walk before it got too hot. There were others out starting their days as well. We were all respectful of the required spacing (six feet), and I kept a mask with me in case the spacing wasn't possible or I needed to go into a store while I was out.

There was a huge difference with that one change. I had accomplished something, been good to myself, and been in contact with the outside world in a safe manner. Now, I could do my grocery shopping and drug store shopping at times when businesses were less crowded. More self-care—check.

When I started to feel bad, I played whatever music I wanted to, as loudly or softly as I wanted. I danced to it, acted out my feelings, laughed at my silliness. Okay, more exercise = feeling better.

My sleep schedule also improved. Yay! After a week or so of this, I could now map out time to think about what I wanted my new life to look like. *Do I want to work another job? Do I want to work a remote job or work and travel? Where do I want to live?* I knew that whatever I decided, I had to be true to myself, doing what made me feel good and satisfying my need to be of service and give back. I started to grow excited about what opportunities were going to unfold for me, though I had no idea what they might be.

I began to meditate again and played meditation music throughout the house. Gradually my angst was going away. I accepted an invitation to take an online Zoom course with a dear friend, and these weekly writing and communicating sessions were life affirming. I was much more at ease, full of laughter, and able to open up to and be with like-minded new friends.

New Sounds

More changes were in store. My lease was up for renewal in June of 2021. My landlord had an emergency with her in-laws and needed to have the condo back so they could be closer. I was given ten days to move. Luckily, my new habits served me well in this transition. I took a lot of deep breaths, reached out to friends, and meditated. Packing and decluttering, though nerve-racking, can be healing. I moved everything I was keeping into my relatives' place and began my new adventure July 4th weekend in a new house, navigating a multi-generational home, and I still had no idea what was to come. I had family to talk to, continued my walking, explored my new environment and its new plant and animal wonders, and kept my earbuds in with music around me constantly.

Within two weeks, I had a call from one of my previous work friends, encouraging me to apply for a consultant position out of state. I was hesitant, but she insisted and said I was perfect for it. Totally unsure, I applied for it and was accepted. My next step was figuring out how to handle living expenses until my first paycheck—about a month. I was gifted hotel points, so I could move forward with the points, my American Express card, and the knowing that I had a month before I had to pay the hotel. Armed with those, on July 26, 2021, I started out on my new consultant adventure. Initially a four- to six-week assignment; it lasted six months—a life-changing six months.

All debt was paid off, and I am now planning my next adventure, using my same tools.

My Sound

How did I get through this?

- Utilizing self-care
- Exercising
- Laughing
- Dancing
- Keeping communication lines open with friends
- Accepting help from friends (huge one for me)
- Meditating
- Keeping music all around me

These practices enabled me to get in touch with my true self, get out of my own way, and to see what was in my best interest so it could shine through.

Do you have any unexpected challenges in your life? You have a myriad of sounds within you to get back on your feet. Any one of the above practices listed under *My Sound* can propel you forward, and I know you will discover more just by taking the first step. The Universe does not allow a void and will show you things you hadn't dreamed of. Your new life awaits. Enjoy every moment and compose your own song.

○

Sharon M. Carrington has a strong spiritual background and loves music, writing, teaching, traveling, and sharing life lessons. She grew up a shy, sensitive person, but now, as a risk taker with an *I can do it* attitude, she was able to navigate heart-breaking life and health situations and come out on the other side thriving. She has a MA in Journalism from the University of Iowa. Connect with Sharon at: soundsofsharon@gmail.com

CHAPTER 8

Mystery of an Altered Reality

Maria Cuccia

D id you know that according to a 1995 Roper Poll more than five million people in America recalled an alien abduction experience at some point of their lives? I am one of them.

I was watching television in my house in 1995, when I heard the words, "Have you, or anyone you know, had an alien abduction experience and struggled to convince loved ones the experience was real?"

I immediately dropped the spoon I was using to eat my breakfast cereal and quickly grabbed a pen and paper to write the phone number that flashed on the TV screen. I trembled when I heard the words: "We want to hear your story." The program was called *The Other Side* and was hosted by an ordained minister and psychologist named Dr. Will Miller. The weekly episodes featured people who claimed to experience the other side of everyday existence. I occasionally enjoyed watching the show because I was interested in such topics, which included psychic phenomena, ghosts, ESP, and alternative healing.

Hearing the question out loud immediately triggered emotions I had buried deep within my soul for many years, and without hesitation, I made the call. A few days later, the producers of *The Other Side* contacted me and asked if I would consider appearing on an upcoming episode along with my husband. They wanted to give me the opportunity to present my story to their studio audience and give him a chance to express why it was difficult to believe my experience was real. My husband assumed the audience would agree that my story was something I had imagined; whereas, I was hopeful the audience would agree something extraordinary truly happened to me. Within a few days, we arranged to leave our daughters with my parents, and we boarded a plane to Los Angeles, California.

The show began with me sitting alone on the stage of NBC studios. Dr. Miller introduced me to the audience and asked me to tell my story:

In 1992, I was thirty-one years old, the mother of three precious girls aged nine, seven, and four, and maintained a strong following as a piano teacher. We lived in a contemporary four-bedroom house on Long Island, New York. We were surrounded by young suburban couples who worked hard to provide the best they could for their growing families. We converted half our garage into a music studio, and I worked from home, teaching children and adults from the neighborhood how to play piano while my husband treated patients at his chiropractic office located twenty-five miles west of our house.

One night in early spring, I woke up from a deep sleep, looked at the clock on my night table and saw that it was 3:00 a.m. My husband was sound asleep next to me. I noticed a strange beam of light shining through the ceiling, and I slowly rolled onto my back so that I could gaze upward and try to figure out what it was. Suddenly, I felt as if I was ascending toward the ceiling at an extremely fast rate of speed as I attached to the illumination. The next thing I remember was standing on what appeared to be some sort of spacecraft with three beings dressed in long, white hooded robes. They appeared to be human, but their hoods covered most of their faces.

One being instructed me to look out the large glass window in front of us. When I looked out the window, I saw many children getting off a school bus. The children appeared to be half human, half alien. One child turned from the group and stared at me. He had a large head with no hair and long thin arms. His black olive eyes locked with mine while he slowly waved his hand side to side. I felt instant love for the boy, and I had a strong desire to hug him, but the glass window kept us apart from one another. With tears in my eyes and an unexplainable feeling of somehow knowing who the child was, I asked the being standing next to me, "Is this my son?"

The answer was, "Yes, this is your son."

I asked, "What is his name?"

The reply was, "His name is Elijah. He was taken from you eight years ago when you were three months pregnant for a good purpose. Someday you will understand this. When it is time, you will see him again. You must go back now, and when you return, look up the meaning of his name."

The next thing I remember is being engulfed in the beam of light again; only this time, I rapidly moved downward until I felt an abrupt pounding in my chest. When I opened my eyes, I was sitting up in bed, shaking and sweating. I heard a voice say, "Look up the meaning of his name; look up the meaning of Elijah."

Although I felt dazed and bewildered, I walked to my bookshelf and found the book of baby names I had purchased when I was pregnant. I looked up the meaning of Elijah and it read: *The Lord is my savior.* I sat on the floor, buried my face in the palms of my hands, and cried until the sun rose.

When I desperately tried to convince my husband that my experience was not a dream, he insisted I see a psychiatrist, which I agreed to do. Unfortunately, I became more agitated when the psychiatrist told my husband I was psychotic and that I needed to take lithium. After refusing to take the lithium, I continued to share my story with friends and family but soon realized how difficult it was for anyone to believe my story was real. When rumors of schizophrenia began to spread around the neighborhood, I feared my daughters would be affected by the gossip, so I made the decision to stop talking about the encounter and keep a journal instead.

After I told my story to the studio audience, Dr. Miller asked my husband to join me onstage and express why he found it difficult to believe me. We were joined by four other guests who shared similar abduction experiences and whose family members expressed reasons why they struggled to believe the stories were real. One member of the audience stood up and cheered me for not going along with the psychiatrist's suggestion to take medication.

The panel included a licensed psychotherapist named Barbara Lamb, who was known for the work she did with people who sought help in coping with other worldly experiences. She stated that although the personal accounts vary with the individuals she has treated, they all seem to share a commonality. She also claimed that the number of people who recalled experiences as indicated in the 1995 Roper Poll was most likely inaccurate because many people are afraid to admit it. By the end of the program, I was happy that members of the studio audience expressed compassion. They conveyed empathy for the other abductees and me as we found it challenging to continue living the way we were prior to realizing our reality was not what we once thought it was.

Dr. Miller concluded the show by suggesting that something extraordinary was happening to many people whose stories had a common theme, and he expressed hope that someday the truth would be revealed.

Although I was grateful for the opportunity to speak openly about my experience on the program, I remained frustrated with the emotions I felt every time I thought about the boy named Elijah. I eventually turned to prayer and meditation to help me cope with my muted thoughts when necessary, and I continued to keep a journal.

The more I prayed and meditated, the more enlightened I started to feel. Once I let go of my fear, confusion, and the determination to understand what happened to me in 1992, I noticed something change inside my mind. I slowly developed a conscious awareness of spiritual messages I believed were somehow being transmitted as mystical compositions of sound.

While focused on listening to the celestial sounds in my mind, I conditioned myself to become aware of the colors and geometric shapes that appeared to be in unison with the vibrations. Heavenly visions slowly drifted in and out, like clouds in the sky. Sometimes I noticed words; other times I noticed numbers and often kept note of the messages and numerical patterns I was inspired to recall. I soon felt compelled to purchase a synthesizer in an effort to replicate the glorious sounds I heard during my states of deep meditation. Within months, I recorded and produced music for healing and relaxation and released music through my own record label, which I named Elijah Records. My CDs became a bestseller for three consecutive years for a distributor located in Hollywood, California, and were voted best new music in a New Age trade magazine in 1995.

Through my turning point experience of an altered reality, I have found peace, healing, and wisdom by journaling and composing music, which has empowered me to reach thousands of people through my work.

I continue to meditate and pray for the boy I was shown in 1992 named Elijah.

If you have experienced challenges that have made you want to bury your emotions, I encourage you to tap into your imagination and creativity. Let go of darkness and pain so that you may unveil your deepest potential. There is no greater gift than the discovery of the true self that lies within the fathoms of your inner spirit. Do not be afraid to pursue whatever brings you closer to resonating freedom within your soul.

◯

Maria Cuccia is the Founder and President of Elijah Records, LLC and Co-Founder and CEO of Advanced Back Technologies, Inc. She has traveled throughout the Middle East, Asia, and Europe. Her story about Elijah has been included in published books, newspapers, and magazines. She has spoken on national television and radio stations throughout the country and is ready to share details of her story through her upcoming book. She is single and lives in Naples, Florida. For more information, write to her at: maria@elijahrecords.com

CHAPTER 9

Red Lights Eventually Turn Green

Ivery D. De La Cruz

Red, yellow, and green are colors used in traditional traffic signals around the world. Red means stop. Yellow means proceed with caution. Green means go, move forward. For some traffic to move forward, other traffic must stop momentarily, then proceed. Just as there are stop and go moments in traffic, there are also stop and go moments in our lives. The stop moments can be turning points where we pivot, then move forward. I share my story with the hope it serves as encouragement when your goals are not being met as planned (stop) and you come to turning points moments (proceed with caution) that lead to your success (green). My turning points moments have led to a greater, more fulfilling life than I could have ever imagined.

Red Light Moments

As my senior year of high school was ending, I did not know what I wanted to do. I was always a good student, a band member, and active in many clubs and activities. So how did I come to the end of my senior year without any direction? I didn't think I would go to college because my family did not have the money. My solution was to join the Army as many of the guys in my class were going into the military. It was 1973. The United States and North Vietnam had signed a peace agreement. The draft was ending, and the United States was moving to an all-volunteer military force. It seemed like a good time to join the Army.

I went downtown and talked to a recruiter who was more than glad to sign me up. Since I wasn't eighteen, my mom had to sign for me. She was worried and my dad's only comment was, "She could be doing something worse." With paperwork in hand, the recruiter picked me up early in the morning and drove to the Military Entry Processing Station (MEPS) for the Armed Services Vocational Aptitude Battery Test (ASVAB).

I felt good about it, although I was a little worried about the folding boxes and the tools. Otherwise, the academic material seemed pretty easy. When the sergeant announced my score she said, "Well, you almost made it. You scored 66. Almost is only good enough in horseshoes." I was horrified. I had never failed a test. I was embarrassed, so this made me think about college.

Yellow Light Moments

I worked part-time in a home for disabled individuals. My employer often told me I should be a nurse. So, I decided to enroll into Texas Woman's University School of Nursing. My sister, who was in college on a full-ride scholarship, told me to contact the financial aid office for help. The Basic Education Opportunity Grant and the Federal Nursing Student Loan Program paid for everything.

My clinical rotations were in the Houston Medical Center, and from the first day, I prayed to never be assigned to MD Anderson Cancer Center. At the beginning the spring semester of my senior year, I looked at the assignment board: Ivery Dotson, MD Anderson. My heart fell. Nothing seemed to go right for me. I was miserable. I cried every day before clinical and felt sick afterwards. Some days I called in sick. I was at the point of stating *I hate nursing!* to which my roommate calmly replied, "You haven't even started nursing, yet."

Finally, I decided to talk to my advisor. Her advice was, "Well, there are other careers you can do besides nursing."

To which I replied, "There is no way I am starting over." After talking to my sister, who had graduated college two years earlier, I dropped the clinical. This meant I had to go another semester to finish. That fall I was assigned to another hospital, completed the rotation, and graduated with my Bachelor of Science in Nursing in December.

Green Light Moments

During that same fall semester, a hospital chaplain requested an intern through the semester missionary program offered by my church denomination. I read the description and knew this was for me. I applied, was accepted, and in January, I went to Louisiana State University Medical Center to begin an exciting adventure learning to be a hospital chaplain. I went all over the hospital, providing spiritual and pastoral care to individuals from all walks of life—in many life and death situations and in happy occasions, such as births and celebrations.

As my five months drew to a close, I was not ready to leave. I requested to continue through the summer. At this point, I knew this ministry was my calling. My mentor Chaplain Fisher, retired Navy chaplain, approached me about a career as a hospital chaplain. This meant I would need to attend seminary and be ordained as a minister.

We talked with the pastor of the church that sponsored me about being ordained for the ministry. This was 1978, and racial integration was just beginning in Shreveport. The pastor gave me a history lesson on how poorly Black people had been treated by this church before he arrived. He gave me a 20 percent chance of ordination. I responded, "Well, it's not zero." We laughed.

That Wednesday night, he brought my request to the congregation. The Women's Missionary Union supported me, and the church voted to license me to the ministry. I was beyond happy as the license meant I could perform official acts of ministry. I heard someone say, "We'll let Texas ordain her" as the seminary was located there. The newspapers and evening news reported, *Parkview Baptist Church has apparently become the first of 34,000 Southern Baptist churches to license a Black woman to preach.*

I was on my way to seminary to study theology, which would take another three to four years. I thought back to my conversation with my college advisor about there being no way I would start over for another career. Well, I now had a new career and was happy to start over. It was worth it.

While in college years before, I had sat in a classroom at the seminary during a missions conference. I thought: *I am coming to school here one day. I'm not a musician, so I can't go to music school. I'm not a teacher, so I can't go to into religious education. That only leaves theology. I wonder if they even allow women into theological school.* Well, yes. They did allow women in theological school. This time I felt joy and excitement rather than tears and depression. I was on my way to becoming a hospital chaplain.

Imagine my surprise when one day I read that an Army chaplain recruiter was going to be on campus. Days before, I had read in the newspaper that at a certain point, the Army was going to be 10 percent female. I told my housemate, "Those women are going to need a chaplain."

I talked to the chaplain recruiter, did paperwork, raised my right hand for the oath of office, and found myself riding downtown with a recruiter to in-process into the Army Chaplain Candidate Program. During our conversation in the car, I mentioned my failed attempt to get into the Army after high school—about the score of 66 being *almost good enough.* He asked when this happened. I told him 1973.

"Oh wow!" he replied. "You needed a 70 to get into the Women's Army Corp." Really! The WAC ended in 1978. All those years, I wondered why the guys were getting in, and I failed. That ride with the recruiter began an almost thirty-year relationship with the Army.

I worked weekends as a registered nurse, so money was not an issue as it was with many of my peers at the seminary. I struggled to get ordained in Texas. One church was afraid I might want to become a pastor one day, but I persevered. Another church, Eastland St. Baptist Church, invited me to be their youth pastor for a salary of $10/week. They ordained me. That $10/week salary helped me meet the criteria for a *salaried ministry position* for active duty.

I graduated from seminary with my Master of Divinity, did a year of clinical pastoral education, got married, came on active duty, and served twenty-five continuous years as a chaplain. We had two daughters; one is now a school psychologist, and the other is a Doctor of Physical Therapy. My husband stayed home with them, and they turned out great. We have lived in California, Germany, New Jersey, Georgia, Korea, Washington, DC, Missouri, and then we moved back to DC where I became an associate clinical pastoral educator, supervising and certifying chaplains for institutional ministry. Finally, we moved back to Georgia where I retired.

After retiring, I decided to give back, becoming a certified classroom teacher through an alternative teacher certification program. Once again, I circled back to my nursing career, took a refresher course, and taught Health Science. Many of my students have gone to college and beyond, touching lives in medicine, pharmacy, physical therapy, nursing, medical assistantship, and many other fields.

Red, yellow, and green traffic lights serve as turning points for drivers signaling whose turn it is to stop and whose turn it is to go. To get to your destination safely, your turning points can be signals to stop one goal and start a new adventure. Enjoy the journey!

Ivery D. De La Cruz is currently a Transformational Life Coach certified by Brave Thinking Institute leading Vision workshops and coaching clients. She is a retired US Army Chaplain Lieutenant Colonel after twenty-five years of active service. During her military service, she was certified as an Associate Pastoral Educator. After retiring, she became a Certified Classroom Teacher. Prior to serving in the Army, she was a registered nurse. Ivery holds a Master of Divinity in Theology and a Bachelor of Science in Nursing. Find out more at: iverydelacruz.dreambuildercoach.com or email her at: iverydelacruz@dreambuildercoach.com

CHAPTER 10

In Hot Pursuit

Dr. Cecilia B. Dennery

Some dreams originate from within. Others come from without, a dream, a calling, a purpose that is so much bigger than you are that it scares you. Such was the case on a warm, 78-degree evening in January 1997. I was living in St. Thomas, Virgin Islands, at that time and had just pulled into the driveway after Sunday evening church service. As soon as I put the car in park and turned off the engine, I heard a voice, clear as a bell, say to me, "Start a Bible school." I was floored. I knew it was God's voice, but I also *knew* He could not possibly be telling me to do such an impossible task.

So I argued. "Why not ask one of the pastors to start a Bible school? After all, they have the resources needed, and I have absolutely nothing."

However, God did not respond to my objections, and so, here I was at a turning point. *What should I do? I am unprepared for this; should I ignore what I heard? Should I pursue it despite my feelings?*

I told my best friend, Gwen, but her response was not what I expected. She calmly stated, "If God gives the vision, He also makes provision."

Those words resonated in my spirit. If the voice was truly God, He would have to make it happen, and that is exactly what He did through a series of seemingly unrelated events. It was early February when I heard a pastor on the radio who was visiting the islands. He spoke so eloquently, I thought to myself: *I would like to meet him*, then quickly dismissed the thought.

That Saturday, I went to the home of Mom Armstrong, one of the church *mothers*. When I arrived, she was entertaining two house guests. After talking with them for a while, I realized there was something familiar about one of the men. I could hardly believe it. That voice! That was the voice of the pastor I heard on the radio that I wanted to meet—and there he was.

I kept in touch with him after he returned to Pennsylvania. In May 1997, I called to let him know that I was planning to visit my brother in New Jersey for the summer and asked if he knew where I could take a Bible class while I was there. He promptly told me about the summer courses offered at Cairn University. After reviewing their catalog, I got excited and submitted my application. By July 1, I had been accepted into the Master of Science in Bible program and was on a flight to New Jersey.

I took six intensive courses each summer for three consecutive summers, completing the degree in the summer of 1999. That was God's provision. I had knowledge of the Bible, but I still lacked money and a facility to start a Bible school, so I returned to teaching at the University of the Virgin Islands.

And once again, God intervened, orchestrating a series of events that changed everything. One Friday afternoon, I dropped in to say hi to Sheila, one of my church sisters who owned a bookkeeping business. She asked me one question after another about the Bible and two hours later, she surprised me and said, "When you start your Bible school, my assistant and I will be your first students."

What?! Only Gwen knew about the Bible school. I stared at her in disbelief. But her next words were even more stunning. "I have an after-school program on the weekdays. I do not use the space on Saturdays. You can use it, *free of charge*, for your Bible school." Incredible! God gave the vision and here was the provision. So I put together a curriculum, announced the start of the school on my radio program, and on March 11, 2000, started Equipping the Saints School of Ministry with thirty students.

It was amazing. I was teaching in my own Bible school. My turning point moment was now a reality. Then a tragedy struck that threatened to abort the school in its infancy. In February, my father-in-law died suddenly. So my husband, Vernon, and I moved in with his mother. That was a difficult time, but we were trying to keep it together. Then, Vernon was diagnosed with prostate cancer. I was in a state of shock. His doctor said they needed to operate. We prayed and cried and prayed some more. They operated on September 13, 2000, and thankfully it went well. I breathed a sigh of relief and was delighted when he came home a few days later.

September 27, 2000, is the date I will never forget. My whole life changed on that day. It was time for Vernon's two-week check-up, so I took him to the doctor's office. I was scheduled to give an exam that day at the university, so Vern told me to go ahead, and he would take a taxi home. So I did. But a few hours later, his mother called me, frantic because Vern had not gotten home as yet, and it was late. I called the doctor's office, and they said he left hours ago. I was worried. *Where could he be? Why hasn't he called me?*

I jumped in my car and retraced the route back to the doctor's office. No luck! I did not see him anywhere. As I was on my way to the house, still looking for him, I got another frantic call from his mother. Vernon was dead.

WHAT?! No! Not possible!

By the time I got to the house, the coroner was already there. I followed them to the morgue. I couldn't believe my eyes. There was his cold, lifeless body on a slab. The cause of death was a pulmonary embolism. He had developed a blood clot from the surgery that traveled to his lungs, and, according to the coroner, Vern was dead before he hit the ground. He did not suffer, but I was devastated—a widow at forty-five years old. I could barely drive back to the house, tears blinding my eyes, numbness engulfing my heart.

As I got out of the car, his uncle came out to greet me and said words I did not want to hear. "The Lord gives, and the Lord takes away. Blessed be the Name of the Lord."

But why take away *my* husband? The family had gathered at the house, but I wanted to be alone. I went to our room and melted. The phone rang. One of my students called to extend condolences. *How did she hear about it so fast?* Then she asked if she should call the other students to tell them that class was canceled for the next night. I had not thought about the Bible school.

What should I do? I didn't feel like teaching. I didn't feel anything. *Maybe I should just close the school. What's the point without my husband at my side? Since God let my husband die, why not let the Bible school die too?*

Suddenly something stirred from deep inside me: *You cannot allow anger to derail the vision. It is bigger than you. It is your destiny. Remember that God gave the vision, and He also gave the provision. How can you give up without a fight?* So I told her, "Please call everyone and tell them we are having class tomorrow night."

That night, every student showed up for class, astounded that I was actually teaching the scheduled lesson on the book of Job. Yes! God designed that I would teach about Job suffering the death of all ten of his children on the same day and how he still blessed the Lord. How could I do any less? And once again, I experienced God's provision. At the end of the class, we formed a circle and held hands. Angie sang and Walton prayed. Everyone hugged me.

By the time I left, my spirit was lifted to a place I did not think was possible. I could see clearly now. Though the road ahead would be difficult, the Bible school and I would not only survive, we would thrive. Yes, I am now in full-time ministry, fulfilling my destiny as president and founder of Doctrine101 International School of Ministry.

What about you? If you are like me, you have also encountered seemingly unsurmountable obstacles that test your turning point moment. For me, it was grief over loss. For you, it might be financial reversals, the loss of a career, a bitter divorce, losing custody of your children, or addiction to drugs or alcohol.

The pearl of wisdom I would like to share with you is that your situation did not come to stay. Losses and setbacks do not define who you are. You can rise above it all because it is only a test. To pass the test, you must press past the pain and remain in hot pursuit of your turning point moment, and then you will watch with awe as your turning point moment turns into your destiny.

Dr. Cecilia B. Dennery, author of over ten books, is a gifted communicator of God's Word. A Bible scholar, she founded Doctrine101 International School of Ministry. Her unique approach to teaching the Word is based on Christ and Covenant as key to understanding the Bible. She is also a dramatic artist who brings Bible characters to life through her dynamic one-woman plays. Buy her books or enroll in a course at: drdennery.com

CHAPTER 11

What's Driving You?

Dr. Felicia Alley English

It looked like an ordinary, sunny southern California day as I started the drive north on the highway that beautiful February morning. I normally set out to drive the straight shot, ninety miles back home—my usual trek those days after my weekends *off*. In that period of my life, I was driven to find safe spaces to relax, to play, to feel magic, and to be alive.

Otherwise, I had isolated, lonely, sad weekends alone. It was all still so raw—a new arrangement, a new way of life, divorce, shared custody, co-parenting, every other weekend without my young sons. Mondays were my day to return to my five- and two-year old sons, whom I worried about incessantly, the house I was fighting to keep during the 2008 housing crisis, and a sadness that engulfed me. Now I was on the road to divorce, adjusting to the shocking news of having a child with a blood disease, hardly working, trying to save my career and sanity. Mondays, after weekends *off*, drove me back to reality.

Without warning, it was no longer just an ordinary day or a usual drive. Suddenly, I began changing lanes impulsively; then everything was hazy. In an instant, I was screaming, weaving, trying to avoid a collision, or worse. While holding the steering wheel in a death grip, my hands were instantly shaking uncontrollably. I looked down, around, outside, then back inside the car again as if someone might be there to explain what was happening. Cars seemed to be speeding by faster than ever—*flying!*

Stone cold sober yet drunk on fear, sweat poured down my face right along with the tears. I searched frantically for a solution, a way out. In a craze, I cried out, "Oh God, please help!" I wanted nothing more in that moment than to get to safety. In the middle of a six-lane highway at the interchange, I was having a panic attack. In that moment, God did help. God took the wheel, and I held on.

Slowly, one lane at a time, I made it to the first available exit. At the first street I could turn onto safely, I pulled to the curb and quickly jumped from the vehicle as if it were on fire. Panting, still in shock, I stared at the car in disbelief. Unexpectedly, I noticed I was holding my hands up impulsively, as if I were under arrest—no fight left, no resistance, no more attempts to control the situation or my life. My body language expressed what my whole being was saying: *I'm done. I can't go on. I don't want to do this anymore.* I was in the universal posture of *surrender.*

What happened? How did I get here, not just on the side of the highway, but at this point in my life—bottomed out, so disoriented, and about to crash? I found myself asking; *What happened?* even though I'd been the one to go through it all—the hills, the valleys, the peaks, the battlegrounds. *What happened to my life?* I knew my story all too well. As a matter of fact, I'd cry out, yell, and pout: *It wasn't supposed to go like that!*

I had cozied up with my story like a security blanket, justifying actions and my inaction. I stayed stuck between angry and depressed, unable to move forward. As familiar as I was with the fine points of *my story* as I perceived it, I didn't know what was really driving me or where it was taking me. That day, I stood there on the side of the highway alone, hands up, a morphed being. I just stood there wounded, worn, fresh from battle, familiar with the surroundings but lost, afraid, and not quite the same.

I didn't fully understand as a lifelong overachiever how suddenly I could be forced to pull over, off the highway (of life) and stop or else. *What happened to my inner strength, my faith, my discipline, my know how?* Sure, I'd been through a lot in the past couple years, but *lots of people go through things*, I minimized. I was taught I should keep driving forward to get through it all. I had dismissed my own needs and denied the weight of the loss, the pain, the hurt, and the fear up to that point; then I couldn't anymore.

What happened to the *make-it-happen* girl who could seemingly accomplish anything she put her mind to simply because she believed and was willing to work to make it happen? What happened to my high resolve, my grit, my resilience?

Fear Factor

"Driven by one hundred forms for fear, self-delusion, self-seeking, and self-pity, invariably we find that we have made decisions that have placed us in the position to be hurt" (*Big Book of Alcoholics Anonymous*, Wilson, 2019). The minute I read this, I related immediately; it instantly explained so much. Fears on every front had overwhelmed me at that time in my life, and I was heading toward a crash mentally, emotionally, and physically. I certainly could have easily died on the road that day.

Fears of all sorts had been driving me to the edge—fear of changes, uncertainty, failing my children, and being unsuccessful. The loss of respect, professional standing, finances, emotional security, safety, and friends also brought fears. I feared being judged and my own condemnation. These fears and more were relentless and driving me to ruin.

I crashed mentally and emotionally there on that freeway from stress and worry, anger and fret, but I was saved from a real *crash and burn.* I was able to walk away. I was freed by my admission of powerlessness and absolutely and completely saved from the futility and fatality of the fight and struggle to figure it all out. I took my hands off the steering wheel, stepped away, and surrendered—all of it, everything. I don't know why in that moment I understood the only truth. The Serenity Prayer famously says it. I had to "*accept* the things I could not change." I recognized acceptance was my only path to peace and happiness.

I managed to call a friend, still shaking, disoriented, and in shock. The only words I could utter were, "I need help."

Yield

What I know today is regardless of how big, challenging, or concerning things get, I don't have to try to control it, fix it, manage it, or run from it. Today, I know that prayer for courage, guidance, and waiting is lifesaving. In each aspect of life—no matter the greatest of unexpected challenges, from pandemic to parenting to profession to provisions—we don't have to be driven by fear. It only leads to stress, ineffectiveness, poor health, destructive habits, dysfunction, dis-ease, poor relationships, and a lower quality of life. The panic attack on the highway was the turning point moment that brought me to absolute surrender. I chose to yield to God, to stop before I completely crashed. Today, I rely more on God's power, not my own, and I practice prayer and meditation regularly. I've learned to seek and wait for direction to address issues and determine priorities, to choose right actions. It is essential to my well-being: mind, body, and spirit.

I was familiar with and taught many self-help programs, but this was different. Even *7 Habits of Highly Effective People* (Covey, S.R. 1989), one of the world's best books, offered valuable information, i.e., scheduling priority self-care in all four dimensions to avoid this sort of crash and burn. Yet I found a spiritual experience was necessary at this juncture, not self-development. I could not fix my *self*. The spiritual shift was learning to trust God, allowing for silence, stillness, and time—waiting for answers versus being driven by my fears in frenetic motion.

Soon after the panic attack on the highway experience I read, "When the spiritual malady is overcome, we straighten out mentally and physically" (*Big Book of Alcoholics Anonymous*). Yes! Exactly! Resentments, fear of the future, remorse, and self-doubt had robbed me of peace. Miraculously, once I surrendered, healing began. Principles like forgiveness, faith, hope, love, and trust surfaced. It was like an instant realignment.

Physical, mental, and emotional manifestations of the spiritual sickness began to reverse—obsessions were removed, stress and anxiety were settled, health issues including migraines and insomnia improved. I no longer desired a drink to calm my nerves, avoid pain, or distract me from my fear and hurt. I had spent four years progressively spiraling down to my *bottom*, but that was not where my story ended. *Bottoms Up!* With surrender, I was granted the ability to get back on the road to wellness and wholeness.

It took some time, a program of action, and most importantly, a renewed, improved spiritual practice to see clearly and move forward on my journey again. *Truth:* Despite things not always going the way I desire or according to my plan, I am safe. There are major detours in life, but I am loved and provided for, always, by my God. People we love die, heartache does happen, sickness and affliction do attack our bodies and minds, and businesses go bust, yet one thing never changes. I can get out of the driver's seat, trust God with my life, take one step at a time, and still have freedom, peace, and happiness along the way.

In the face of calamity, uncertainty, and distress, remember these words that literally appeared on a sign from God for me one day when I needed it most: "I know the plans I have for you . . . not to harm you, plans to give you hope and a future." (Jeremiah 29:11, NIV). What looks like failure, collapse, or the end on an ordinary day can be God pulling you over to yield and realign.

Ask yourself: What's driving you? I hope you choose to yield when signaled. Pause and pray often. Enjoy the gift of meditation. In the silence, God speaks. May you listen and be guided in your life—home and personal, business affairs, and endeavors—as you proceed on your purpose-filled journey.

Dr. Felicia Alley English is a Speaker, Independent Sr. Learning and Org. Dev. Consultant, and Executive Coach. Felicia joyfully serves the Optimum Health Institute, SD/Austin, and in prior years, proudly served the FranklinCovey Co. as a Training Delivery Consultant, facilitating 7 *Habits of Highly Effective People* and additional content. Dr. English's clients also include business and educational leaders (principals) whom she teaches powerful strategies to "Lead and Live Well." To work with Dr. English or pre-order her upcoming book, *Bottoms Up*, visit: DrFeliciaEnglish.com or connect with her on LinkedIn.

CHAPTER 12

Choose Love

Colleen Flanagan

What I did not know when I made the decision to follow through with an unplanned pregnancy was that I was about to embark on a journey that would fulfill my purpose for *being*. This was not an easy decision. As a single, professional woman who had lost both parents to cancer in my mid-twenties and with no offer of support from the father, I was frightened at the prospect of raising a child on my own. In addition, I was still reeling from a crisis of conscience, having terminated a previous pregnancy against my religious beliefs and values at the time. I knew in my heart that the choice to terminate this pregnancy was no longer an option for me. This time I listened to my heart and chose love over fear.

Having worked in the human services field for years serving people with developmental disabilities, I was determined to do all that was necessary to ensure that my child was well-cared for in the womb, as well as after birth. I followed all maternal health guidelines. When I began cramping and spotting a few months into my pregnancy while attending my sister's bridal shower out-of-town, I sought medical care at the local emergency room. There, I was attended by a wise physician who shared this poignant message, "If this pregnancy is meant to be, it will be."

Though initially put off by this expression, the words resonated deep within and began shifting my awareness from the outer to the inner world of being. I relaxed into the knowledge and acceptance of what was true. I became acutely aware of my child's presence; I tuned in and connected on a whole different level. I knew then that this child was, indeed, meant to be. I felt I had been chosen as the vessel to carry, nurture, and usher this unique being into the world. I recognized that there was a divine plan greater than my current understanding and embraced this child whole-heartedly.

Unable to return to my studio apartment with an infant, I brought my daughter home from the hospital to my brother and sister-in-law's home until I could resettle. Having delivered her fifth child just three days before my daughter, my sister-in-law was a great support and calming influence. We both received welcoming gifts for our children. A friend of the family had sent a plaque to my sister-in-law with the following message:

There are only
Two lasting bequests
We can give our children—
One is Roots,
The other Wings.

Once again, I was struck by poignant words that resonated deep within—being shared with me as an offering. I no longer felt alone in raising my daughter. I was being guided along the way by the Universe. All I needed to do was remain open to receiving the messages and trust my own knowing.

Easier said than done. As a young child, I did trust my intuition and escaped from a potentially dangerous situation, only to be chastised for having been in the situation at all. My freedom to visit and entertain in the neighborhood with songs and dance was cut short, and I retreated into a world of imaginative play. Though this had its rewards, what was lost was a trust in myself and others. As my life proceeded, my decisions were often made out of fear of repercussions or a mistrust of others. Choosing to have my daughter reaffirmed that inner voice as my true voice. The voice that saved me years ago was now my redemption. My faith in myself and the Universe was being restored.

My daughter continued to inspire and authenticate that voice. Her mere presence in my life has challenged me to show up and be accountable in every moment. I began exploring the root causes of my own life choices and discovered strengths I didn't know I had. I faced fears I didn't know existed and embarked on a journey toward wholeness—a journey that is ongoing.

As a bright, curious, and inquisitive child, she would often question my decisions or the reason behind my requests. Rather than telling her, *Because I told you so*, and entering into a power struggle, I would reply that I was just following the mother's handbook. This response seemed to satisfy her, and the truth is I was listening to my own inner wisdom, borne of a mother's love.

Over the years, she has inquired as to the presence of this handbook. I shared that she would receive her own guide when and if she became a mother, for what I know now is a mother's love is about a heart and soul connection that is a gift from the heavens in the form of a child.

Years later, my young professional daughter invited me to brunch to celebrate Mother's Day and gifted me with a card thanking me for raising her consciously. She inquired as to how I had managed to steer her away from bad influences and choices that would be harmful to her well-being. I shared the *Roots and Wings* quote, realizing that it had become my guiding principle in raising her. My intention was always to allow her to find her own voice, rooted in the knowledge that she was loved unconditionally.

Deep in my core, I understand we are gifted children to become all they are capable of becoming, while holding them in the bosom of love and protection. They are not ours to possess nor are they here to live out *our* life's dreams. They are gifted to us so we may support and guide them toward becoming who they are meant to be. How miraculous is it that it is equally an opportunity for us to realize our own potentials?

While helping me sort through some memorabilia and journals one day, my daughter discovered that I had terminated a pregnancy prior to her birth. When I confirmed that this was true, she turned toward me and simply said, "Well, I came anyway!" Her gentle wisdom continues to astound me. Gratitude for having been chosen fills my heart. I no longer believe there are any mistakes in this world.

Over the ensuing years, I have been gathering materials, quotes, and memorabilia to create a unique Mother's Handbook for my daughter. I have a message to share. It may not be new, but I think it bears repeating, if for no other reason than to remind other mothers that we all struggle with achieving a balanced approach to deal with the *push and pull* of parenting. The message is: *You are not alone.* Our wisdom lies within. Creating this book has become my life's purpose as it will be my offering to the world, my way of paying it forward for the gifts I've received.

My daughter recently gifted me with a grandson. He exudes joy. This is our natural heritage. Unencumbered by the conditioning that occurs as we become citizens of the world, he just lives in the moment. I watch my daughter interact with him in the most loving manner, allowing him to explore his world while ensuring he is safe and protected. Their heart connection is apparent, and I get to experience grandmother love.

When I chose to have my daughter, I chose love. I have gained a deep appreciation for all the turning point moments in my life that have allowed me to evolve both spiritually and emotionally. I now trust these moments are for our benefit if we stay open to the lessons they hold. I have learned lessons of forgiveness, perseverance, hope, and resilience. Most importantly, I trust my own knowing once again, holding the sincere belief that I am protected by the Universe.

When you can move beyond your fears and your limiting beliefs, you are able to respond with your heart. When you follow your heart, you will always choose love.

A friend recently exclaimed, "If love is the answer, then what is the question?" Choosing love simply means: Listening with an Open heart to the Voice of the Eternal wanting to be expressed for your well-being and the good of humanity.

Life is all about choices. You are offered myriad opportunities to choose your own path. The question is: Will you follow the path of least resistance, following the crowd without thought or intention, or will you choose the path of love? It is not always the easy path. It requires mindfulness and discernment and sometimes facing your own demons, but it is a richly rewarding path.

Choose love.

○

Colleen Flanagan is first, and foremost, a mother. She has extensive education and experience in child and play development. However, she attributes the inspiration she received from a simple quote about *Roots and Wings* and her deep spiritual connection to her own wisdom as the guiding principles that informed her while raising her daughter as a single mom. At the request of her daughter, she is creating a mother's handbook based on her experience. For further information visit: AMothersHandbook.com

CHAPTER 13

The Dragonfly Princess and the Manager

Karoleen Fober

I felt troubled. I was on my way to savor some decadent treats at my favorite chocolate store with my husband, and all I could think about was this nagging, recurring issue having a silent war in my head: claiming my supernatural gifts—*all* of them.

I had been having conversations about this issue with myself over and over for months. I was frustrated and getting nowhere. I felt desperate and needed guidance, Divine guidance.

My conversation with God that day went like this: "I'm so happy to be serving You in this wonderful way, and I love helping people with their life struggles and times of loss. But, I'm scared. What will people think of me? Will they take all this the wrong way? I'm afraid my relationships would change with some friends and family members if they knew. You know how some people don't believe there are those gifted with Your supernatural gifts. And so many ignore and disregard their own intuitive abilities. Some people act like I'm a bit too much anyway, with my heightened intuitive abilities and sensitivity. You know what happens. They get quiet, their eyes start rolling, everyone feels uncomfortable, we move on to something else, and I end up feeling defeated. You know how much I hate to be rejected. All I want to do is help people and serve You."

There. I poured it all out: the good, the bad, the ugly scary, and the stuff I didn't want to admit. That's the thing about God. He lets you do that. He lets you be weak before he reminds you of your strength and His faith in you to do what's right and to serve Him for the highest benefit of all, letting Him handle the naysayers.

I took a breath and waited.

The answer was clear as His answers always are. *It's time*, I heard. Then, *How are people going to know you can help them and others if you don't claim this additional gift I have given you and tell people you are a medium?*

When God speaks to me through the Holy Spirit, I am always humbled.

I gave myself a silent pep talk to stop worrying about what others think. Besides, He was right. I needed to work on keeping my focus on helping people. God would take care of me and the non-believers.

"Okay, God. You are right, and I promise I will start telling people."

We had just arrived at the chocolate store, and I went to the counter eagerly. After my Divine intervention side bar, I was feeling like these calories were going to evaporate as I enjoyed every bite. Yep, I was feeling invincible.

I was their only customer. I noticed a beautiful, multi-colored dragonfly tattoo on the neck of the young woman waiting for my order. "What a beautiful tattoo!" I exclaimed.

"Thank you. My mom and I got the same one together."

"That's so neat! I think some tattoos are so beautiful, but I would never do it because of the pain." I shook my head and shuddered.

She said both she and her mother never experienced any pain while they were getting their tattoos.

"That is quite a phenomenon! While I have never experienced that one, I do experience other phenomena."

"Oh, what kind of phenomenon have you experienced?" she asked.

There it was—my open door. Would I go through it or hold back in fear again? I took a breath, and said rather quietly, but clearly, "Well, I am a medium."

Her eyes opened wide, and her eyebrows shot up near her hairline. She covered her mouth as if she were going to scream. She twirled around and started looking in the back area of the shop. Suddenly, the front door swung open, and four customers walked in.

I thought, *Okay, I've scared her, and she's looking for the manager to throw me out.*

I called out that I didn't want to bother her and went outside where my husband was waiting. He was on a call, so I sat melting in the heat of the Florida afternoon wondering what to do. When I saw the four people walk out of the store, I decided to go back into the air conditioning, and I promised myself I wouldn't bother the young woman. I would simply get my chocolate treats, sit down, and cool off. That's it.

I walked back into the store. Now there were two women standing behind the counter. The one with the dragonfly tattoo was pointing at me and jumping up and down. I asked God to please help me as I didn't want to be in trouble.

As calmly as I could, I started reading the menu, trying to focus on the chocolate. The new gal said, "Are you a medium?"

I felt myself beginning to choke, but fought it, and said, "Yes."

With a big smile, the new gal explained she was the manager. I relaxed. I could tell they were simply hoping for a nugget of wisdom for their life. I willingly obliged.

The dragonfly princess went first. I shared that I was being told she was a healer and that she should start the instruction she desired. She responded that she was hoping to become a nurse but had been hesitant about applying for school. She expressed relief and gratitude for the Divine confirmation she'd just received.

Then, her friend, the manager, started talking. I interrupted her, "Oh, you have *two* questions for me."

She said, "How do you know that? Because I do have two!"

I smiled, pointed, and looked up. "I just know!"

I then said, "Okay, we'll start with the most important question in case twenty people walk in and we have to stop the reading."

She said, "Should I get a divorce?"

I frowned. "That doesn't sound good or right."

Suddenly, to my right, a beautiful female energy appeared. I said, "Wow! Whoever she is, she has tremendous power and strength." I felt my right hand rise and point to the manager's husband as if he were standing there next to her. The female spirit was wagging my index finger at the invisible husband like he was in real trouble with her.

It was an accident. Not her fault. I heard the female spirit proclaiming.

The manager exclaimed, "Yes!" She started trembling and holding her face in her hands.

I then kept hearing the name, *Bobby,* again and again, so I said, "I'm not sure what this means, but I keep hearing the name Bobby over and over—Bobby, Bobby, Bobby."

The manager paled as if she had seen a ghost. "How do you know my son's name?"

I said, "I don't, but this female spirit does. She wants her son to start thinking of her grandchild and to stop blaming you—because you are innocent."

I pieced together that the manager had been in a car accident seven years ago that was clearly not her fault. She was driving with her baby son and mother-in-law in the car. The mother-in-law protected the baby in the car and died doing so. The husband blamed the manager for his mother's death. Bobby was now seven years old, and the manager had suffered under relentless and misguided blame from her husband for seven long years. The best solution she could think of was to divorce him, break up her family, and try to stop the despair that was slowly strangling her.

I don't remember buying or eating the treats I took home that afternoon.

But I'll never forget the dragonfly princess and the chocolate store manager. Watching the tears stream down the manager's face, I thought about what would have happened to this woman and her family if I had not promised God that I would claim the gifts He'd given to me. How much and how long would she and her family have continued to suffer?

While we can never really know the difference our gifts will make in other people's lives, or how they will be received, I was grateful I had decided to not hold back that day.

Are you holding back your Divine gifts? We all do at one time or another. But there comes a time when we must face our fears. I was afraid of what others would think. Some of us are afraid our gifts aren't good enough. We compare them to others and discount their value. We may think our gifts need to be practiced and aren't quite ready, or we are afraid of making a mistake.

But, when we focus on our fear, we're focusing on the wrong problem. Remember there are people who need your help and guidance right *now*, and they don't need you to be perfect. If you have been holding back, isn't it time you claimed your gifts and started taking steps toward helping the people you were born to help?

○

Karoleen Fober, Intuitive Business Coach and Medium, helps heart-centered entrepreneurs and Light Workers leverage their intuition and manifesting abilities to fulfill their Soul's desires to serve. Contact Karoleen at karoleenfober.com to learn about her offerings and forthcoming book on Divine Intervention and to discover how miraculous events guided Karoleen through her life to reach her Soul's mission today.

CHAPTER 14

Cracking the Shell of Fear

Liliane Fortna

When I decided to contribute to the *Turning Point Moments* anthology, I was convinced the serious health challenge I faced a few years ago, including its positive outcome, was my turning point moment. That experience led me to write a transformational book to help others use their innate ability to see and interpret signs and synchronicities.

For most of my life, I have felt compelled to help people. I believed my serious illness was the catalyst motivating me to share an approach that will allow people to lead better, richer lives. I was pleased with this idea and wanted to use it as the focus of this chapter.

Nonetheless, as I started writing, it hit me that my book was not the end but the beginning of a new venture—the platform, the pulpit from which I can spread the message enclosed within the words. The more I thought about it, the clearer it became that I should not hide behind my book but fulfill my calling by personally delivering my message.

However, I had a couple problems. First, the word *marketing* elicited tremendous *fear* in me: fear to have a presence on social media, fear of constant contact with people, and fear of speaking in public. It's not a new aversion; it was present all along. But when I started writing the book, I felt I didn't have to worry about it until much later in the process. Although I understood that a book doesn't sell itself by magic, I thought I'd still get good results by doing the minimum required.

There was a second fear. In my book, I share personal experiences I had always kept to myself. To open up and discuss many episodes of my life that I'm uneasy talking about—this is out of my comfort zone.

It's not that I have never been in the public eye. Over the years, I have had extensive and varied interactions with the public. Regardless of where I lived or what I was focusing on, my urge to help people was a constant:

- I taught dance and exercise to seniors to bring fun in their lives and help them improve their balance, memory, and spatial awareness.
- I taught fun, creative dancing to very young children to prepare them for ballet class.
- I trained models.
- I taught image and fashion to help men and women improve their self-esteem by learning to develop a confident image of themselves in their personal and professional lives.
- I felt comfortable giving speeches on fashion to large groups and organizing and presenting fashion shows.

Although these were fun and rewarding activities, I still felt something was missing. Deep inside, I knew I had more to give. I just didn't know what.

After years of persistent nudging from the Universe, I finally accepted that it was time to start training as a healer. I embarked on several years of studying with traditional healers and shamans in Europe and the US. As I started on this new path of inner discovery and consciousness awakening, I discovered aspects of myself I had overlooked or taken for granted all my life. And beyond this inner growth, these new skills also became a way for me to reach out and help people more powerfully than I had done before.

Then, I had to face a frightening health situation. After nearly two difficult years of uncertainty, the path to recovery was remarkable, causing me to reflect on my entire life. It was a fantastic voyage inward where I was able to revisit events I hadn't understood at the time. Many forgotten episodes of my life vividly resurfaced, and I felt transported to when they happened. I knew I had to share my stories and the messages I was receiving.

During my month-long stay at the hospital, I had plenty of time to reflect and start writing all that was coming to my mind and my heart. I knew my life would never be quite the same. It became crucial for me to write a book to help others use the innate abilities we all have but gradually lose as we grow up. I thought this was my turning point, leading to my legacy—an illness leading me to write a book that would help others even after I'm long gone.

As I was writing this chapter, however, the publication and launch of my book were growing closer, and I had to face my fear and dislike of marketing.

I reluctantly signed up for a LinkedIn account, activated my author's website, and created a private Facebook group. As I approached the time when I had to ask my friends for help regarding the book launch, I started to feel physically sick. At first, I didn't realize what was happening. I thought maybe the stress of the holiday season and other events were responsible. I couldn't sleep at night. Violent headaches woke me up, and sometimes I felt a heavy weight on my chest, couldn't breathe, and was drenched in sweat. My headaches became so frequent and violent that I had to see a doctor who ordered an X-ray and sessions with a physical therapist.

Soon, I felt the shell of protection between my fear and me developing spidery cracks.

Gradually, I realized that this painful period was a time of transition. I had been in transition before, and each time it was the harbinger of something significant occurring in my life—a major change, a birth, or rebirth of a part of me. It was humbling to realize that even though I'm a healer and the author of a book about seeing and using signs from our guides, I had failed to recognize what was going on until the physical agony became too intense to ignore. My fear of having to promote my book on social media and possibly give live presentations or interviews was so strong that it overshadowed the path my Spirit Guides were trying to show me.

Nonetheless, more cracks appeared throughout the protective shell.

Transition is never comfortable, and it often heralds changes we're afraid to face. In my case, the actual reason was fear of not being able to express myself verbally in a coherent manner. True, I had been in front of an audience many times. It always made me a bit nervous, but it was not paralyzing. This time though, in my book, I reveal some deeply personal experiences I have never talked about. The thought of publicly discussing these episodes frightened me. Deep inside, even though I knew my book's message was important to share, I had doubts about how well I could express myself.

I realized my dilemma: Do I sit back and hope my book sells itself, or do I become active and face my fear to deliver the words I painstakingly put on paper? In today's world, we're gradually moving away from receiving information solely via books. Many people don't read much anymore and prefer to learn via videos, audiobooks, or any form of social media. My book alone might not reach all the people I want it to.

A battle raged inside me. On one side, the fear of failure to express myself verbally was paralyzing, and on the other side, I knew that it was the right way, the only way for my message to reach the maximum number of people. Once I realized this inner turmoil was making me sick, I started to face my demon.

Spidery cracks started to spread.

I jumped into developing my website, Facebook group, and LinkedIn account. I shared a .pdf version of my book with friends who agreed to help me with the launch. Their kind words of encouragement and their excitement warmed me to the idea that marketing could be fun and not as scary as I saw it.

Spidery cracks now covered the entire shell.

Then, an amazing thing happened. I experienced a moment of truth at a dinner party I reluctantly attended. My hesitance to go was mainly because I knew people would ask about my book, and I was afraid I couldn't discuss it articulately. Well, what a surprise! Everybody *did* want to know all about it and told me how proud they were of my having done it. I found myself comfortably answering all questions.

My protective shell shattered, setting me free to bring my message to the world—without fear.

The metamorphosis is such that I just signed up to become certified to teach transformational seminars online and in person. This will be a perfect complement to what I intend to teach through my book. My husband even decided to join me on this new venture and will also get his certification so we can work as a team. What a change! Who would have thought the message of my book would lead me to this point?

You, too, can crack your shell.

Most of us have created protective shells to insulate ourselves from pain, grief, uncertainty, and fear of failure, when in fact, we're isolating ourselves. Yet, if you can summon the courage to peek through the cracks, you will find not only a different world but also your true self, full of wisdom and hidden treasures that need to be shared with the world.

So go ahead—emerge from your shell and be free.

Liliane Fortna is the author of *Winks from Above*, a transformational book. She is also an energy healer, having received her education in Europe and the United States. Previously she has been a professional dancer, European fashion model, fashion consultant, and Amazon rain forest explorer. French Vietnamese by birth, she grew up in France and has lived in England, Norway, Italy, Germany, Belgium, South Korea, Japan, and now the United States. For more information, visit her website: winksfromabove.com

CHAPTER 15

A Paycheck for Myself

Dr. Kim Gebron

We grew up with my mother working three jobs to support us during the 1960s. I began working the day after my sixteenth birthday for a local grocery store, and this money helped with household and my teenage expenses. I worked through high school and college, beginning a full-time job immediately upon college graduation. Yet even with a decent salary, there was never enough money to put aside into savings after paying bills and my school loans. Emergencies, such as unexpected car expenses, meant using my credit card and increasing my debt.

My first full-time employment was with a small privately held business that conducted energy and environmental research and development projects. One payday, the company president told us there were insufficient funds to cover our paychecks.

Ten years later, I switched industries and entered the world of sales.

Fast forward to the year 2000. I was working in a high stress, executive level position with a new pre-school photography company. The owner spent an entire year recruiting me. I felt ready to jump into a C-level position, even though I had a fulfilling job as a sales trainer and senior sales representative with a well-known national day care photography company I will call Forever Kids Photos. Although my earnings were not great, my job was fun, and my clients knew and liked me. But, there was nowhere within the business for me to professionally grow.

It was a horrible mistake to take the new job with "Digital Pix."

Within the first month, the owner reneged on the salary he promised. He interfered with the business plan we developed and overrode a majority of my operational decisions without discussion. I had recruited 70 percent of the company from personally known business associates. They came because of my professional reputation and integrity in the industry. The majority of them were angry as they left lucrative, established careers to be employed with this new venture. The associates I recruited felt overworked, and two thirds of them quit. Half of them permanently cut off contact with me. I lost business credibility.

My prior employer was upset I left. The owner of Forever Kids Photos, for whom I had worked directly, was so angry he never spoke with me again. My current pay was much less than promised, I was working longer hours, and I felt as if I was sinking fast. I would lie in bed at night, unable to sleep. My stomach was in knots; there was an acid taste in my mouth. My primary thought was: *What have I done, and how can I undo this?*

Months passed, and we encountered more challenges. Digital technology was in its infancy; our photographic images looked digitized with green hair strands and inferior quality. Editing took hours. Customers complained. More people quit. We jumped from fire to fire, solving immediate problems—which eliminated our time to plan, create systems, and execute our ideas.

After six months, I heard from Ray, a former business associate. He was my original mentor in the school photography business. He had more than twenty years' experience in the industry, and he was responsible for my opportunity to work for the largest national daycare photography studio, Forever Kids Photos.

He suggested we meet for lunch at Denny's. While eating, he recommended we open our own preschool photography company. I will forever remember this point in time. I listened to his proposal thinking: *How can we do this? I do not have sufficient savings to invest in a startup. We do not have the equipment we need to begin. How can we hire people without money to pay them? How can this succeed?* There was self-doubt, fear, and an overwhelming belief that we could *not* make this happen.

Yet, with all those questions and thoughts running through my mind, I replied, "Yes, let's do this!" Instantly, Pinehurst Photography was born.

During that lunch, we selected our company name and decided on each of our responsibilities. I would create the legal structure, manage the money, market, and find new accounts. Ray would source and obtain the equipment, hire and train photographers. He would also create the sets, build props, and coordinate with the processing lab. Both of us would share the task of selling the finished product.

We talked daily and met regularly. I signed up fifteen schools within the first two weeks for test sessions. In the beginning, it was only Ray and me. He was the photographer, and I was the account representative. I put in long hours, still stunned we were in business together. I realized I was doing the same thing I had done for three other companies. The only difference was I was doing it for our business, not someone else's.

Nancy Lynn, a friend of mine, loaned us $20,000 for startup capital. We purchased photography equipment and marketing materials and paid the photographers we hired.

The day arrived when Ray photographed our first school, the Navarro YMCA Child Care Center. There were over forty children. Two weeks later, I was at the school to show and sell the portraits. It was just as

I had done it in the past except—when I sold the first package—I stood there in shock, holding a check payable to our own company, Pinehurst Photography. At that moment, I experienced a major turning point in my life. This epiphany was so strong, so literally Earth-shattering for me, I can still visualize myself over twenty years ago.

I was sitting behind a child-sized table in a child-sized chair. We had enclosed the portraits within individual transparent plastic bags displayed in columns on the table with every child's face visible. Our package and pricing sheets were on the sides of the portrait package. We offered three package sizes and individual portrait pricing. It was noisy, as are all childcare centers, and the children knew their parents would soon be there to take them home. It was a chaotic and stimulating, yet a comfortable and familiar environment.

A jean clad, T-shirt wearing father in unlaced, dirt-encrusted construction boots came in to pick up his son. He stood about 5' 7." His hair was deep brown; he was in his twenties. I said hello and invited him to look at the pictures.

Most fathers walk by our table during the picture sale day, knowing their wives or mothers will stop by later to decide what to buy. This father removed his son's portraits from the bag. He sorted out the poses, looked at his smiling boy, and selected the mid-size package. He wrote a check, made it payable to Pinehurst Photography, and handed it to me. I thanked him, and he left as I stared at the check. It was at that moment I realized I could work for myself and *generate my own paycheck*. I could develop whatever programs I wanted, set pricing, select the marketing campaigns I wanted, establish my own quotas, and sell the way I chose rather than following a scripted dialogue.

I photographed the check, made a copy, framed it, and hung it in my office until I sold the business.

This began my full-time entrepreneurial game. The thrill is still present every time I generate payment from a client. I have started five businesses since then and sold three.

My partnership with Ray lasted approximately two years. We had remarkable success during those initial years, starting from zero and selling more than $350,000 within the first twenty-four months. We established offices in four cities and employed twenty-five people. During 2021, I came across the photos from our first company-wide meeting as we entered our second year in business. It was a bittersweet memory. I thought about how focused and enthusiastic we were, the lives we impacted, and the families who still carry the photos we took in their wallets. It gives me chills to realize the portraits we took are framed and hanging on walls as a memory of a child who is now grown.

Ray left our company and began his own. Our business relationship soured, and unfortunately, our parting was not on the best terms. Years later, we had a short phone conversation, and our paths have not crossed again.

As I reflect on the turning point I experienced during our first sale, I realized another occurred while writing this chapter. That turning point is forgiveness interlaced with gratitude. Without Ray's mentorship and friendship, I would have missed the happiness I experienced during my twenty years in preschool photography. He initiated the conversation and action for creating a business that exists today.

That experience led to some inquiries that became interwoven with how I have approached life since we began Pinehurst Photography. I ask myself these questions, and I encourage you to ask yourself similar ones as you face your own turning point moments: What course of action can I take, and what is the impact it will have on other people? Does my enterprise or action put something good out into the world? Am I grateful for the people who work with and for my businesses and do I acknowledge them? Am I a good mentor to those who wish to grow?

A simple conversation at Denny's changed and expanded my life into becoming self-employed for the rest of my career.

Dr. Kim Gebron is a serial entrepreneur who has experienced many turning points during her life. Kim began several businesses, including American Word Pics, Forever Classic Portraits, and Drawer by Drawer. She lives with her husband in Texas. They are avid animal rescuers who enjoy a household full of Shih Tzus and cats. When she is not creating new businesses, Kim likes to read, attend the theatre, collage, play bridge, and spend time with friends.

CHAPTER 16

Bee Love

Sherry Gesner

It was a beautiful fall day in October 2014. I was driving down one of the main roads in my hometown when my cell phone rang. It was my husband John, asking where I was as he had some news about a doctor visit. We were both traveling in the same area, so he asked me to meet him in the parking lot of our church. Two weeks prior, my husband had gone to see his primary doctor to have an odd symptom checked out. He was attending a local college and was enrolled in their accelerated adult program to obtain a business degree. He had noticed his handwriting was slipping badly while taking notes. His physician ordered an MRI. The doctor suspected a possible mini stroke. *Perfectly manageable,* we thought, if caught early.

I was closer to the church than he was, so I pulled up into the mostly empty parking lot and waited. My husband arrived shortly thereafter, pulling up alongside me. We both rolled down our windows. He said, "Dr. Larry's office called. They made an appointment for me with a neurological oncologist next week."

Oncologist, wtf! My mind started spinning. I could see the fear in his eyes. I shoved down my own and remained steady in my gaze, trying to reassure him that we didn't know anything. "It's going to be okay," I said, hoping and praying I was right.

The next week, my husband and I were sitting in the neurological oncologist's office, looking at the X-rays he'd pulled up on a screen on his desk. "A brain tumor?" my husband asked.

"It's a grade 4 glioblastoma; it's terminal," explained the doctor gently. He went on to explain the location of the tumor on the parietal lobe and its size.

"How long do I have?" my husband finally asked, rubbing his hands up and down his thighs.

Dr Muhammad replied, "The normal prognosis for this type of cancer is less than five years."

The feeling of shock was palpable in the room. Time stopped, and I felt like I couldn't breathe. I forced myself to focus, breathe, and be present for my husband. I reached for his hand.

The doctor proposed surgery to remove as much of the tumor and surrounding cells as possible, followed by chemotherapy in pill form and radiation. The doctor explained if my husband decided that he wanted the surgery and treatment, then he wanted to schedule him for surgery the following week.

We went home and talked about it. We were determined to do all we could do to prolong his life. John called the doctor and asked for the surgery to be set up. He contacted personnel at the hospital where he worked for benefit and leave information. I contacted my employer and was granted family medical leave to take part of the day off to drive my husband to and from his radiation treatments and to work from home the rest of the day.

Due to the sensitivity of brain surgery, there was a possibility there could be seizures after the procedure. John called his attorney and had his will and power of attorney completed, handing the envelope to me when he came home. I was sure I wouldn't even need to look at this for years and years. I had decided my husband was going to be fine. He was going to beat this, and we would get back to living our normal lives. We were hoping to retire early in several years, do some traveling, and enjoy life growing old together. I had lost so many people already; surely, I wouldn't lose my husband too. I was confidant he was going to be okay. I didn't realize I was in complete denial.

My husband's surgery was successful in that the surgeon was able to remove all the visible tumor. He completed the radiation and chemo. We changed our diets and ate better; family and friends were supportive. Eventually, he started his classes at the college again and went back to work and church and spending time outside.

John loved the outdoors and was a beekeeper. He had several hives and would head out the door saying he had to check on the girls. Our daughter Mary and I helped bottle and label the jars of honey for sale. We had a stand at the end of the driveway with honey bears and bottles on it and a cigar box with a small amount of change in it for folks to drive up and buy honey.

It was almost two years to the day, in October 2016, that the doctor found another tumor on the opposite parietal lobe. Another surgery was scheduled. John was so strong and fought so valiantly for his life regardless of personality changes, brain fog, and fear. His family meant everything to him. My husband lost his battle with brain cancer in January 2018, at age fifty-nine.

I was devastated and fell into a deep numbness, going through the motions but not really being there. I had read a story once of a woman wailing and wearing black after her husband died. I never understood until my husband died what that really meant, what she must have been feeling. I found myself wailing and rocking at times, sobbing so deeply I could barely breath. *We had so many dreams yet to live.*

Most days, it was a chore to drag one foot in front of the other, but I had to go to work, and I had a teenage daughter who needed me. I couldn't succumb to the deep grief and let it drag me under too far, for too long. We went to bereavement counseling. It helped, but I stopped going to church as it was too painful. My husband's larger-than-life presence was there. He sang in the choir. He was always helping where and when he could, and everyone loved him. I felt the numbness in myself, but there wasn't anything I could do about it. I was in a holding place it seemed, a self-preservation mode.

Eventually, I knew I had to do something. I could feel my vital life force slipping away. A woman I met randomly started a conversation with me and shared that she had lost her husband a few years prior. She shared a meaning of the word H.O.P.E. with me. She said it stood for *Hold. On. Pain. Ends.* She hugged me, and I hugged her back in deep gratitude. The love and kindness of my family, close friends, and at times, complete strangers blew me away. I started following a few spiritual teachers and hearing messages of comfort and love.

Finding my own way, I started doing yoga, walking around the neighborhood, and journaling. I allowed myself to feel the feelings I had numbed and started integrating them. I took classes and training in different spiritual modalities and embodiment practices. I listened to podcasts and watched videos. I started feeling better and growing stronger. I focused on what I needed to do for my own self-care, being loving to myself, and healing from the inside out. I became certified as a spiritual advisor.

In feeling like I had been turned upside down and inside out, I learned to surrender. By going within and being present and compassionate with myself, I was humbled. I touched the soul and found deep peace. As seasons pass and new seeds sprout, the grass grows green again, and hope is renewed.

Though still finding my way, I'm walking forward toward new life and new love, step by step, honoring my process. One of my teachers says: *Just be love. Just be the love that you are.* Love is all there is.

My husband, the beekeeper would have said: *Bee love. Just bee the love that you are and dream new dreams.*

○

Sherry Gesner was born and raised in central Ohio. She is a mom, grandmother, and great-grandmother. Retiring after thirty-two years in finance, she dove into healing and spiritual studies. She enjoys that first cup of coffee in the morning, watching the sunrise, spending time at home and with family and friends, listening to music, dancing, road trips, train rides, reading, writing, spending time in nature, her cats, and sharing smiles. In her free time, Sherry can be found scoping the city for gluten-free goodies. Sherry can be reached at: sherrygesner369@gmail.com

CHAPTER 17

Look at Me

Rebecca A. Glassing

Why does society become uncomfortable or tend to act differently when we see someone who has a handicap or a disability? This is a question that is easy, yet difficult to answer, a question I ask myself every day.

When I am filling out medical paperwork, for example, I am asked to answer some of the following questions: full name, weight and height, age, medical history, and ethnicity. The question that is not asked is: *Can you see?* It is exceedingly rare that I am asked this question by the nurse. Yet, when I go in for an appointment, I need to tell every person I interact with that I am legally blind. You might think this should not be important; however, this is of the utmost importance for me.

Once I tell someone that I am blind, our interaction will fit one of the following scenarios.

If I am lucky, the other person continues to treat me no differently. They may ask me for a little guidance, so I can ensure we both are getting what we need to make our time successful. Or I may find that the other person really does not know what to say or do to assist me. This again is okay. When someone is honest with me, the moment becomes a teaching experience for me to educate them on assisting someone who is blind or has low vision. It becomes a win-win opportunity for everyone involved.

In another scenario, my interaction with another is not successful. This lack of success ends with me being ignored, them speaking over me, or them talking to the other person with me. This situation has and continues to happen to me on a regular basis.

This last scenario has made losing my vision hurtful and frustrating. I never was asked if I wanted to go blind. I was never asked if I was willing to have to deal with daily obstacles. I was never asked if I was comfortable with always needing to ask another person to assist me with simple tasks that sighted people take for granted, nor was I ever asked if I wanted to live in a world where other people seem to think that it is okay to ignore me since I am not able to visually see them.

Fifteen years ago, I was diagnosed with a non-cancerous meningioma brain tumor. I would have surgery to remove it, recover, and go back to life as I knew it. No one, including my surgeon, could have ever known that after this surgery my life would never be the same.

What was supposed to be one surgery turned into a total of three surgeries, all within a forty-eight-hour time frame. I crashed twice, three of my skull bones had to be removed to allow my brain to expand from the massive swelling, and a large blood clot developed, causing me to have two strokes, which in turn, damaged my occipital lobe and caused me to lose my vision.

Recovering, adjusting, and learning how to live in this new world was not easy. It was not until I was at a check-up with my surgeon, Dr. Gregory, that my entire perspective changed. I asked him what the survival rate was for what I went through. He told me that to survive all three surgeries, the survival rate was less than 1 percent of 1 percent, and statistically, I should not even be sitting there talking with him. It was then, after the initial shock, that I realized that I would never complain, nor would I ever be angry about losing my vision. This was bigger than me, and there was a reason I survived. What that was I was not sure.

I was lucky enough to be brought up in a home with parents who came from two diverse backgrounds and were raised differently from one another. My father was raised on a farm and was the tenth child of thirteen. He attended school with students who all had remarkably similar backgrounds. My mother, however, was primarily raised by her grandparents in a neighborhood of St. Paul. She grew up with people from many diverse cultures and religions. She went to school with people who were Catholic, Jewish, Lutheran, and others, people who came from white, Black, Lebanese, and Mexican cultures.

My parents used these differences as a teaching opportunity as my brother and I grew up. They taught us to treat others as we would want to be treated. Out of all the lessons that my parents taught me, this is the one that truly resonates for me today.

When my extended family and friends learned about my vision loss, I did not think that I would be treated any differently. To my surprise, I was overwhelmed by all the numerous ways they responded. I thought about one of my favorite poems, "A Reason, a Season, and a Lifetime," by Brian A. (Drew) Chalker. This poem talks about how people are always coming in and out of our lives—some for a brief time, some for a specific reason, and others who are forever in our lives.

It took me time to fully comprehend all that was changing in my life; however, I eventually chose to fully grasp this reality—that not only were my interests and needs changing, but the people in my life were changing as well. I came to realize that it was okay to say goodbye to people and relationships, knowing that it was time to start a new chapter, to make room for the new experiences and people I would be welcoming into my life.

If I had not gone through trauma with the brain tumor and lost my vision, I know that I would have not experienced some of the best times I have had since then, like canoeing and camping down the Namekagon

River in Wisconsin, winter camping on the edge of The Boundary Waters Canoe Area in Northern Minnesota, as well as doing a Tough Mudder.

Being able to camp again brought back an activity that I loved and did on a regular basis prior to losing my vision. It gave me that sense of freedom I was missing in my life, while at the same time enabling me to learn and experience new activities, like canoeing, dog sledding, and snowshoeing, regardless of my vision.

Participating in a Tough Mudder obstacle course was something I never thought I would find myself doing, let alone in the mud. Yet here I was with members of the gym I belonged to, taking part in this craziness. This was even trickier, considering I was doing this blind. Knowing that this was going to need some creativity on my part, I reached out to others in the blind community to see if anyone had done anything like this. I was excited when I connected with others who had done similar races. They passed along many tips to make my experience a little easier.

Along with my good friend Rachael, we went through the obstacles in tandem by connecting our arms together with a rope. This allowed us to continue the course without any need for my white cane. Even though we had signed up for the full race, we realized early on that we would only be able to finish the half Mudder. By the time we finished, we were completely covered in mud, laughing hysterically, and I experienced one of the best things I have ever had the opportunity to do.

People hear about these trips and other activities I participate in and question how I am able to do so without my vision. What I say to them and to anyone who asks me is this: *I am no different than anyone else you meet.* Yes, I may have some restrictions and need to make some adjustments; however, this does not mean that I am not able to do the same as others. No one has the right to take away my will to thrive in life, nor does anyone have the right to make decisions for me. I have a brain and know my limits, so please let me be the individual God created me to be.

The love and support I continue to receive with all that I do is so encouraging and uplifting. I have learned that even without my vision, if I continue to challenge myself, step outside my comfort zone for new experiences, and most importantly, believe in myself, I am just as strong, if not stronger.

Instead of mourning the life that I *lost* at the age of thirty-three and looking at all of the *what ifs*, I now embrace what is ahead of me on this new journey. I have this whole new world that I get to explore and to show people that anything is possible regardless of personal challenges. I have been given a great opportunity to educate and broaden those who are not familiar with the visually impaired community.

I can be a role model for those who may think that because they have a disability, mental or physical, that they *can't* do what everyone else is doing. Instead, I have the chance to show them that even though they may not be able to participate in the same way as someone else, with some adjustments, they still get to have the experience—it just may look a little different. I know every person I cross paths with provides an opportunity to know that in some way, I have made an impact on their lives. This is a gift I get to share.

Always remember to treat others how you would want to be treated. If we can all remember these words every time we meet someone new, each of our paths will become more enriched. You never know, the next person you meet could be someone with a vision loss who has a lot to share.

○

Rebecca A. Glassing lives in St. Paul, Minnesota. She is a brain tumor survivor and volunteers with the American Brain Tumor Association (ABTA) on their yearly BT5K fundraising event. She also volunteers with WELS Mission for the visually impaired where she transcribes various documents into braille. To learn more about her journey or to contact her, email her at: glassreb2022@gmail.com or visit her CaringBridge site at caringbridge.org/visit/rebeccaglassing

CHAPTER 18

The Dance of Light and Shadow

Elizabeth Grace

I am not sure how long I lay in that space of welcome numbness sprawled on the floor—no feelings, no thoughts, no boundaries, no reference points, no identity—just floating in an ocean of endless nothingness. I was an empty vessel, tired and spent; there was no fight left in me.

Who was that woman? Why was her Light so diminished and how did she end up on the floor? That was me. When I think of it now, it seems like light years ago, a different life and a different me. The woman I have become allows me to see that time through a different lens as a distinct and powerfully transformative moment in which my life changed. This was the moment I vowed I would never again abandon myself, give away my power, dim my Light, or acquiesce just to keep the peace. I would never again show up as the woman I had been.

It was 2012, the year the world was supposed to end or change its ways. It seems that this Mayan prophecy echoed in my life. It turns out I did both: my old life ended, and I changed.

I thought I was happy, that I had the perfect life: a wonderful loving husband, two great kids, a nice home, and the freedom to be a stay-at-home mother to raise our children. I thought: *I'm lucky and I should be grateful.* That was the story I told myself every day. I could show up as a happy woman in the company of others, but I could never shake this underlying tension in my body and mind. I was miserable and couldn't understand why. I lived inside that paradox for years. I was so confused, and it was draining my life energy. Just after our twenty-fourth wedding anniversary, I knew it was now or never. I needed to leave or disappear forever, lost to myself.

I packed up my little car. It was a beautiful sunny day with a vivid blue sky and one tiny heart-shaped cloud that drew my attention. I took it as a good omen. I arrived an hour later at a cottage close to the beach. That night, I lay looking at the ceiling, listening to the different sounds, exhausted and grateful, trying to quell the rising fear in my belly now I had finally done it.

The last words my husband had said to me were, "Go and sort yourself out. I'll be here when you get back." I translated this as: *I'm the one with the problem. There is something wrong with me that needs sorting.* He was obviously fine and didn't need sorting. I needed to understand what had happened to two good people who came together in good faith that we could have a happy life together. We had both done some personal growth training and some spiritual studies. Yet, one of us was miserable, and the other had no idea that something was deeply wrong.

As the days turned into weeks, my happy bubble of relief started to deflate, and anxiety began to take up residence. I was anything but sorted. I knew I couldn't go back, not yet, maybe not ever. I had become skillful at stuffing my feelings away in a cupboard somewhere in my subconscious. However, the cupboard was so full I couldn't close the door anymore, and feelings were escaping, tumbling out in waves, swamping me. I was being haunted by everything I had hidden from the world and myself —sadness, grief, anger, fear, resentment, and loathing. I was coming undone, losing any sense of reality, and subsiding into the abyss.

Then one day it happened. My legs buckled, and I collapsed into a heap. There I was on the floor, no sense of time passing, finally depleted. I had nothing left in the tank, no brain cells firing, nowhere to go, and no stories to tell myself.

After what seemed like an eternity, I began to feel quite peaceful. Fear and panic had left; guilt and shame were nowhere to be seen. I was just a speck in the vastness of life. Eventually, I became aware of dappled light playing on the walls. I watched, mesmerized by the beauty and perfection of the dance of the light and shadow. I was excited by that thought. Heck, I was excited I had a thought. A new energy was coming into my body, an energy not directed by me. I was just the observer witnessing sensations returning and spreading through my whole body —gentle yet powerful, peaceful, and purposeful. It felt as if Life was engaging with me again and an opportunity was presenting itself.

I knew I had broken through some barrier but had probably experienced a mental breakdown. My whole nervous system shattered into a million pieces. I lost touch with reality, my world imploded, and I was scared out of my mind. Literally.

This was a gift. Because my mind was suspended and not accessible, neither were the stories I had on repeat:

- *I am incompetent.*
- *I am a bad wife and mother.*
- *Life is unfair.*
- *God has abandoned me.*

This new mental space allowed me to re-centre myself. I wasn't dying; I was just recalibrating.

I knew I had married a good man whom I discovered had dysfunctional beliefs and behaviours around women, relationships, and marriage. We were born into a culture in which a man naturally has access to his wife's body when he wants, regardless of her wishes.

"A man has rights," my husband said to me once, and in my dire lack of self-esteem, I agreed with him. It didn't even occur to me in that moment that I had rights too. It seemed our unconscious cultural conditioning had dovetailed. I tried to talk about it, but he dismissed this issue as my inadequacies and high expectations and somehow twisted it into something else. I was so disconnected from myself, I couldn't even articulate clearly. I felt hammered into submission, which seemed easier than fighting.

There was never violence, and the worst verbal abuse was him stating I was a lousy wife. However, the impact on my *beingness* was profound. I felt unseen, unheard, deeply misunderstood, betrayed, abandoned, objectified, and violated. I began to loathe his touch. The disconnection from myself and from him had grown acute. I felt like caged prey, and unfairness and resentment circulated within me, creating deep schisms in my psyche. I knew if I didn't leave, I would die. My Soul was screaming at me to leave.

On the floor in the dappled light of the cottage, I began to ask: How had I allowed this to happen? How had I co-created this mess?

The answers began to come. I was so weakened physically, emotionally, and mentally from enduring stress for so long I hadn't been able to make any sense of it or to make a stand for myself. I could see I had essentially abandoned myself. That thought was almost too much to bear. I sobbed until I had no tears left.

I began to feel so much love and compassion for this part of myself that had been stuck in a story that was grafted onto me through marriage.

I recognised how I helped perpetuate this pattern—what I'd allowed, feelings I'd squashed, my ongoing capitulation, and the stands I didn't take—and I took responsibility for it all. In that action of self-responsibility, I was no longer the victim. I was no longer someone my life happened to; I put myself back in the driver's seat. I recognised I had the ability to create change. The relief I felt in my body was palpable.

I began to forgive myself for abandoning and judging myself, for not knowing how to make a stand, for holding so much anger and resentment in my body, for not believing my voice was worthy of being heard, for forgetting that I am divine and precious, and for forgetting that I matter.

Eventually, I found myself grateful for the situation and everything that led me there, as this allowed me to begin the journey of coming home to myself. I now knew, without a shadow of a doubt, that I would never abandon myself again. I was now fierce in my stand for myself and other women.

***

What if your uncomfortable feelings are trying to tell you something, a symptom of a deeper misalignment with who you truly are? What if you could work with them to get to the truth of what is going on?

Do your beliefs about yourself make your life easier, happier, healthier? Beliefs are not necessarily truths. They are usually passed on to us by others in our lives we deemed authorities, including the media.

Are you trying to stuff feelings away somewhere you can't feel them? By not allowing your feelings to be expressed and heard, you could be silencing your own inner voice. What if turning towards them instead of away from them could be your first step?

Most of our uncomfortable, scary feelings are generated by fear or by misunderstanding parts of ourselves that are stunted through something that happened when we were not old enough to understand. Bring your compassion and kindness to this part of yourself: you've been through a lot, and it's understandable to feel this way. Reassure yourself that you will witness and acknowledge your own strength and courage. It's safe to speak now.

What if our uncomfortable feelings are a call for recognition, for love? With unconditional loving and acceptance, these parts can be integrated back into your beingness, and you will become wiser, kinder, more confident, and energised on your journey home to wholeness.

Become your own best friend, and no matter what comes your way, be kind, love yourself, and dance to your own tune of light and shadow. What if you are the one you have been waiting for?

Elizabeth Grace has been researching health and consciousness for over thirty-five years and has worked in the fields of environment, health, and education. She graduated with studies in natural systems, and in 2010, completed her Master of Spiritual Science. She is a workshop leader, speaker, and trained Feminine Power coach, facilitator, and leader. Elizabeth runs Soul Circles for women who seek to live their best life. She is the author of *Return to Wholeness* to be published in 2023. Contact her at: simplelivingnow.com.au

CHAPTER 19

7000 Jars of Jam

Nancy Griffin

Everyone has a mother, and I consider myself to be one of the lucky ones who had an amazing mom. My Mom was a pioneer in her time and the catalyst for countless turning point moments in my life. Some of them were so subtle I didn't notice them until decades later, while others were profound in the moment.

My mother, Margaret Evelyn (Wilson) Robertson, was born in 1907. I was born in 1949. This was probably my first turning point moment because my Mom was forty-two years old when I was born. This gave me the blessing of growing up with an older and very wise, progressive mother.

My siblings and I called her Mom, but everyone else called her Eve. When I was only twelve years old, in 1961, she launched her homemade preserves and jam business.

In the early '60s, women's roles in business and in the workforce were defined by cultural notions about women's appropriate role in society. This *cult of domesticity* held that women could best serve the political and social needs of the country by dedicating their energies to the creation of healthful and nurturing households. This idea shaped popular perception about what types of jobs and occupations were proper for women who needed or wanted to work outside of the home or family farm—but not for my mother, who was a trail-blazing entrepreneur right from her kitchen.

I consider her to be a *Prime Time Woman*. I first heard this term spoken by Marti Barletta at a Women Presidents Organization conference I attended. Marti described *Prime Time Women* as women generally aged fifty to seventy whose families are grown and gone, housework is done, and menopause has flown out the window. These women have the attitude: *Now I am free to be me*. My mother was one of those women. Not only did she start her business in 1961, but I grew up under her expansive and progressive influence as she also became a stock market investor and mini philanthropist.

Yet, prior to that, she truly was an excellent homemaker in more ways than one: baking, cooking, handmaking her family's clothes, upholstering and refinishing furniture that she bought at local auctions, leader of 4H, president of the Women's Institute, member of the Eastern Star, member of the Baptist church, and in her later years, an active duplicate bridge player. The *Leave it to Beaver* life was the norm, and my mom was *Mrs. Cleaver* in farm country until 1961.

Unwilling to settle for less than what she dreamed possible, she started a homemade jam business. She initially sold her products in local stores and off the front porch of our farmhouse. As demand grew, she approached larger markets who agreed to place her products on their shelves. Her business grew consistently because customers loved what she was creating—a 100 percent pure product with no additives.

In addition to the businesses that stocked her products consistently, she grew her base of loyal customers by fulfilling personal orders and by offering local business owners a gifting service for their clients' special occasions. She particularly enjoyed these business customers as she was incredibly creative, loving bright colours and design, so bringing these aspects of her talents forward for her customers was something she deeply enjoyed. On Maslow's hierarchy of needs, her level of self-actualization was extremely high; she loved what she was creating in the world, and her creations were appreciated by many people.

Accomplishing this in the '60s was certainly a turning point moment for her, and I realize that being up close to witness my talented and determined mother was also a turning point moment for me.

For Eve, things just kept getting better. With some of the profits she earned, she started to invest in the stock market. This new adventure was something she pursued proudly and wisely. She always researched the investments she was considering and subscribed to two financial papers, which came in the mail.

Through these subscriptions, she learned more about business by reading about different companies and what made them successful. She particularly enjoyed the stories about the CEOs and the unique ways they led their companies. I believe it was her own powerful leadership that allowed her to appreciate the leadership styles of other successful people.

I picked up this practice from her, and it has impacted my life in significant ways. I've grown my own business partly because of what I've learned from the business leaders I've observed—another subtle turning point moment from my mother.

Remember, Eve started her jam business with no loans, no advice, no support, no mentors, and no local group that supported business initiatives or entrepreneurship, especially for women. However, she moved forward by her courage and drive to take a risk, getting in the game, creating something unique that she enjoyed, and making her product so good that people could taste the quality difference of her jams. She truly loved making and sharing her jams with everyone who knew her.

Eve received many compliments —both for her product, and her *gumption,* as she would say, to start her own business. She was a rarity back then, and people truly appreciated who she was and what she created. Think about the risk she took of losing her money or not being successful. Also, there was another risk for her at that time—the societal risk of stepping out and trying something new and different. So, she managed that additional pressure as well.

Over time, my mother grew her business with two part-time employees helping with the jam making production. Eve always put the labels on each jar herself—quality control to the max! She was particular about each label being perfectly straight; she prided herself in having a *good eye* for details. She was proud of every jar she produced, and the final reward was that perfect label on that jar to be enjoyed by some happy customer.

Having Eve as a mother taught me so much: the importance of creating something of quality, caring about clients and customers, taking risks, and breaking society's molds. I hope you see how these gifts of my mother can help you in your life as you navigate your own turning point moments.

As if all of that wasn't enough, my mother was also musical and played the family piano well. In her investment research, she read about a new Canadian piano manufacturer. She admired the CEO and his business, and that inspired her to buy a brand-new piano—a large purchase made with incredible pride—because it was *her* money that paid for the piano. Even now, long after my mother is gone, the piano is being enjoyed by her granddaughter Julia and her two great-granddaughters, Cara and Gabi, who take after Eve in the musical talent department.

My mother was also an early supporter of Women's Resources, an organization that helped women displaced by domestic violence. In this way, her work created turning point moments in the lives of so many women, and I'm so proud of her for helping these women.

I want to share one final jam story involving her biggest customer. Eve's business was seasonal, and she normally received orders in the late winter for late spring delivery for their busy tourist season, and in the early fall for the busy holiday season. With this particular jam order, she had not heard from her regular buyer, even after following up several times. This was unusual, and she grew quite discouraged.

She decided she'd go *straight to the top* and typed a letter to the CEO, asking for his help, which she mailed on Tuesday after Canadian Thanksgiving weekend, Oct. 1990.

In a twist of fate, Eve died suddenly early Friday morning that same week. She died of a heart attack the day after the doctor had diagnosed her with indigestion, a common misdiagnosis of heart disease in women. We were all shocked, as we had just seen her the previous weekend and she was feeling well. Even at nearly eighty-three, she was still going strong. This was the last thing we expected while awaiting a response from the CEO for her jam order.

Sure enough, we received a letter in the mail the following week, saying that there had been a big redo in the department where the jams and preserves were sold. The company's buyer had said *yes* to everyone, and it had become a mess of too many orders. That buyer was transferred elsewhere, and the new buyer was told to pick the top three sellers and to let the rest go. Eve's jams were picked as one of the top three sellers, so even after her passing, her delicious high-quality products were still in demand. This was a bittersweet moment for all of us and a turning point moment as we experienced the power of her legacy firsthand.

After the order came in, we told the CEO that she had just died suddenly, and he felt terrible. Thanks to my incredible mom—who had anticipated an order from this customer—we were able to fill most of the order from inventory already in stock. I told my Dad that when he died and saw her again to please tell her, *We got the order!* She was in the top three and would have been thrilled.

To build on Eve's legacy, my Dad, three siblings, and I, started an "Evelyn Robertson Young Entrepreneur Award" for an eighth-grade student at the local public school for a student who had taken initiative to start a small business. Eve especially appreciated young people with gumption.

What I learned from Mom is ingrained in me, and my own business, Women, Worth & Wellness has many elements of who she was, what she valued, and what she reinforced. When I think of my mother, I think of Betty Friedan's quote from the '80s: "Who knows what women can be when they are finally free to be themselves?" My mother answered that question for herself and has inspired me—and perhaps you—to do the same.

○

Nancy Griffin, CFP, EPC is a connector and influencer. Nancy attributes her success to personal courage, determination, and joy, when focusing on women's health and wellness, hence creating Women, Worth & Wellness® in 1994. Nancy enjoys every opportunity to inspire and inform women about their personal health and wealth, net worth and self-worth, philanthropy and legacy—so that women feel fabulous, generous, joyful, confident, and on *top of their game* every day. Visit Nancy on her website: womenworthwellness.com

CHAPTER 20

Born This Way

Lynardia Groubert

For sixty plus years, I carried a deep sense that my natural way of being in this world at birth had been altered at an early age. The memory of that moment was buried deep inside me, and there was always an underlying question of what had shifted and why. My parents never mentioned any questionable incident other than my birth was a difficult delivery for my mother.

Once I was old enough to no longer nurse, I was relocated to my grandparent's home. I carry no memories of this, but I do have a deep, innate knowingness of crying for my mother. My grandparents, parents, and I lived that way until my brother was born two years and eight months later. I could see in photos that holidays were spent at both my parents' house and at my grandparents' house.

I remember the awkwardness of my life upon being reunited with my parents and a new brother and the emptiness of no longer being with my grandparents other than during our Sunday visits every other week. The absence of my grandmother—whose bond and presence to me was undeniably my one constant—was horrific. Everything known was now unknown, and the uncertainty of my life loomed before me, causing frightening moments of insecurity and aloneness. I remember asking my mother why I lived at Grandma's house.

Her answer, "Oh, your father and I thought it would be best as we were working so much." Even at five years old, the answer seemed vague. My curiosity was further piqued when my brother was not separated from our parents during his early years.

Life settled into a normal pattern that was seasonal in Ohio. Spring was planting season. I loved the feel and smell of the freshly tilled soil and the plantings of seeds and tiny plants. Summer was filled with nurturing the plants that would provide the food we would be harvesting in the fall, and winter was when the soil was readied for next year's growing season. Yet, as these times of family connectedness were rich and sensory, within me there remained nagging questions about my early years. There was a feeling deep inside me that I was different in some way that made my parents not want me.

As a child, I discovered dance—the movement, the music, the flow—and I felt happiness for the first time. Dancing helped me cope with the nagging feeling that something was *off*, and my mother did not want to speak about it. Throughout my adolescence and college years, my mother chose to continue her silence.

In college, I discovered the beauty of architecture and design, the natural flow of materials and substance to a beautiful finish. During those studies, my own natural flow of desire yearned to awaken the true nature of my soul, but the old questions of my early childhood were still present.

In 2005, my friend, Sarah, recommended a book. Glancing at the cover, it was written by a female shaman of the ancient traditions of the Western Andes. I had gained a deep respect for shamans who had crossed my path during my tenure with tribal communities, so my interest was piqued. I devoured the book in a weekend and instinctively knew that meeting this shaman was paramount in uncovering my truth.

Once I located her, I reached out to see if there was a possibility to work with her. After a bit of time, she said yes, and I began my journey with her in Santa Fe, New Mexico. Her teachings were rich; the ceremonies were deep dives into myself. The process was deeply emotional on every level, leaving me drained and weary. While her guidance brought me close to my early childhood events, the final breakthrough to my deepest truth remained locked within.

When I think of her, I am reminded to be patient, practice the ancient teachings and ceremonies, remain curious, and be the love that I am.

It was only a few years ago that my awakening incident happened in a most unexpected way. While visiting a dear friend in Santa Fe, New Mexico, we decided to take a nature walk. During the walk, my friend asked why my left hand was curled closed. His words flooded my brain, and immediately I realized the information that was buried so deeply was about to move from its inward shelter into my present awareness. My mind was so flooded; I do not remember if I answered him that day.

In the days that followed, I was consciously aware that my left hand was curled when I awoke every morning. It felt natural and comforting to have it curled. Furthermore, any time I was relaxed or in my natural flow, my left hand would curl. I started a practice of self-love every time my attention was drawn to my curled left hand. I would slowly uncurl the fist and bring my open hand over my heart and let my heart's love flow into my palm. Many *whys* later, the memory unfolded and the difficult answers to the questions I had carried for decades were revealed.

The Truth: At an incredibly early age, before my mind had any knowledge of set patterns, my mother believed it was unacceptable for a young lady to be left-handed. And, of course, I was born left-handed. The separation from my parents was a time for redirecting the functionality of my left-hand to my right-hand. My left hand was bound, thereby forcing the use of my right hand. I was moved to my maternal grandparents' home fifty miles away from where my parents lived to prevent public scrutiny.

As I grew older, the binding was removed for set increments of time during the day, or until my left hand tried to take its rightful place in my life, which then brought the binding back into place. I now remember the gallons of tears that were shed. Grandma would hold me on her lap while kissing the tears away and loving me. I have memories of her love and her promises that everything would be wonderful soon. And then, one day, the binding was no longer needed; the battle of wills between my left hand and my right hand was complete. That is when I moved home with my parents and baby brother.

To this day, there are things that I am unable to do with my right hand, and there are things I can do with either hand. And to this day, my left hand will curl when I am most relaxed. Inviting the truth into the flow of my life was not easy, but there is finally a peaceful acceptance and connectedness of how this changing from left hand to right hand has worked on my behalf and not on my behalf. The extraordinary gift of truth has enhanced my life's journey to be whole.

If you live with a constant internal knot that is triggered by the words of others or your own thoughts or feelings of being *less than*, trust in your courage to follow your quest for truth. You will find the strength and perseverance to uncover or unfold that which is hiding within you.

Remember you, too, are worthy of *living in the beauty of love.*

○

Lynardia Groubert is a forthcoming author and spent most of her career in the corporate world creating environments by mentoring individuals and teams to navigate the intricacies of group and corporate self-awareness. Her long personal history of bringing her own personal dreams to life, including her quest in finding her wholeness is based on her tag line: *If you can dream it, we can make it happen*. She attributes her success to being prepared for the unexpected, while anticipating the unknown. Lynardia can be reached by email at: Lynardia@gmail.com

CHAPTER 21

Creating a Life You Love by Finding Love Within

Rosie Guagliardo

We sat there like any typical Saturday night at a lively, new restaurant in the city. It always felt so fun to be out with my husband. Although we had been married only a little over a year, we had been together for about a decade—since we were nineteen years old. We grew up together.

For several months before this moment, I could feel something was off. Even more recently, I thought I knew what the issue was between us. I was desperate to figure it out, and then, once I thought I knew, I needed him to tell me the truth; I needed to hear it from him directly. Actually, he needed to be able to tell me.

And finally, the words came out. "I'm gay."

I put my hand on his arm and assured him, "We'll get through this together."

And then, we cried. We cried for what felt like months. I thought I'd never laugh, smile, or be happy again.

How can love bring such pain? We all know it does, but love is so worth it. From that moment on, I decided I wanted to lead from love. I've always been loving toward others, but it came with a cost. I'd lose myself. I'd put others' needs and desires before mine. That's when I realized love really needed to start with me and for me.

So, I set out on a path to love myself. It sounds trite and like it should be an easy endeavor; however, it felt anything but after one of the most devasting relationship moments in my life. There was so much resistance—more than I even knew. I hope in sharing my story of how I did it, you too can feel love for yourself and let it radiate. This will allow you to love others more fully on your journey. From this place, I know you can create a life you adore too.

After my husband shared his truth, we felt paralyzed and couldn't imagine our lives without each other. Not only did we have to separate, but he had to share his truth with the world in a time when it wasn't easily accepted. With my response, I had hoped to set the precedence for how anyone should respond to him. If I—his wife and girlfriend of ten years—could accept him, I felt like anyone should be able to do so. However, we had the reality of the world to deal with.

So, where do you start when it comes to loving yourself? By being true to yourself.

Allow me to introduce myself. I'm Rosie Guagliardo, a beauty-seeking, lover of life, Italian-American who is pragmatic, purposeful, and goal-oriented. This dichotomy has always been who I am. However, for many years, I realized I wasn't allowing my whole self to shine through. Parts of this woman would come out in a measured way at the *right* time or with the *right* people.

Some would have said I was highly self-aware. I'd say I was worrying that I wasn't good enough for anyone. So, I was hiding parts of myself, showing up fragmented, and playing this juggling act constantly trying to prove myself—leaving me exhausted, tense, anxious, and always thinking: *I'll be happier when I have a loving husband, a nice home, and a fun and successful career.*

Fast forward a few years to the beginning of my story. My hard work had finally paid off. (So, I thought!) I lived in a cute condo overlooking the lake with my loving husband, had a fun job, vacations, and more. From the outside, it appeared as if I had it all.

But I was still exhausted as I continued to chase new, different goals this time, like a fit body, that next promotion, and more love from my husband. I thought I had to work even harder to get anything I desired. I was in constant survival mode, trying to get everything done, and I wasn't really experiencing what I dreamed to have in my life.

My divorce became my turning point. I had to stop hiding parts of myself and over-engineering my life, hoping that when I had everything perfect, I could live with ease and grace. It was time for me to be my true self and have that version of myself take full responsibility for making myself happier.

Finding Love Within

I began exploring what I really wanted and embracing who I was completely—the good and the bad. I started sharing the real me—my strengths, what's important to me, what I repress, and my deepest wishes. I began looking for and appreciating perfection—the beauty, the lesson, the love—in me, relationships, and in every moment, knowing that life is happening now and that my circumstances will never be perfect or just right.

Creating a Life You Love

Here's exactly how I did it by incorporating the following principles in my life.

Set an Intention

I set an intention during my divorce to live daily with grace and dignity. I wanted to put my head on my pillow at night knowing I showed up this way no matter what happened. It wasn't easy, but that inspired me every day to act in a way that I knew would get me the results I desired.

Connect with Inner Guidance

I didn't tell anyone about our divorce for six months. I wanted to respect my husband's privacy and wait until some family festivities and holidays passed so I wouldn't ruin them. Many said I was strong for waiting to share. But the truth was I didn't know how to be true to myself yet and not take in others' opinions. Plus, I felt like a failure because I couldn't see that our marriage wasn't working.

So, I needed to build courage to share this truth. I went back to prayer. Although I grew up Catholic and it was a big part of my Italian culture, I hadn't prayed for years. I knew I couldn't ask to change my situation, so I prayed to feel peace so I could share my truth, especially with my family. I started by telling my siblings, who gave me 100 percent support.

When the day came to tell my traditional Sicilian father, I prayed harder. My sister prayed with me, not knowing at the time that we were both praying for the same thing—a feeling of peace. (This reinforced my belief in the power of numbers.) As I drove to see him, a wave of calm came over me. It felt magical and came at the perfect time. We met eyes, and he gave me his big, warm smile. He already knew and accepted me fully. It was such a gift to feel peace in my heart before, during, and after that moment.

Practice Gratitude

With each change that occurred during my divorce—from moving into a smaller place, to separating bank accounts, and changing my last name back—I committed to practicing gratitude. It wasn't easy and didn't happen right away at times. But it happened. Instead of thinking: *I'll be losing my beautiful duplex condo, Mercedes, and luxurious vacations to places like Bali*, I focused on how I'd have a place that was much easier to clean, I didn't have to worry about parking that nice car in the city, and I'd find other ways to travel to faraway locations. Within a few months, I booked a trip to Sydney, Australia. Who knew?

Find Simple Joys

Maybe most importantly, I had to find my joy. For the first time in my life, I really tuned in to what I wanted in the moment. My first night of living alone, I was ready for dinner. The choices were limitless since I didn't have to consider what anyone else wanted. Letting others decide what they wanted for dinner had been my way to put other people's desires first. So, I decided to microwave popcorn. It was the most delicious popcorn I had ever eaten.

Create a Values-Based Vision

Eventually, I created a vision for my life that felt all mine: one that was based on my values and inspired me daily to wake up and go for what I wanted, one that pulled me forward versus one I was forcing to happen. I began trusting it would all come to pass as it should and that every opportunity presented to me was a chance to learn and take my next right step in life.

With these principles, I began to accept and trust myself. I allowed the real me to show up. That's when the transformation happened. I attracted people, situations, and opportunities that aligned with my deepest desires, and I created a career I love, a focus on wellness that energizes me, and relationships that light me up.

Are you ready to create a life you love? Then, I advise you to consider the practices I have described. Set intentions for every moment of your life and definitely for big moments. Connect with your inner guidance. Then, be sure to trust and receive that information.

Also, remember everything in life has the meaning we give it. So, practicing gratitude reinforces the theory that the narratives you tell—about yourself and your situations—shape and form your life. Be sure to focus on empowering stories.

Ultimately, I learned I can't control my life circumstances, but I have a choice about how I show up and the energy I radiate in the process. This journey of connecting with my true self helped me love myself and others more deeply and to be inspired to realize my life vision with ease, joy, and grace daily.

Rosie Guagliardo is the founder of InnerBrilliance Coaching and has been a certified life and career coach since 2007. She combines her Northwestern psychology degree along with her coaching certifications and eighteen years of advertising experience to help her high-achieving clients discover an easier way of living in which they can experience results with joy and grace. Her holistic and pragmatic approach helps people generate, revitalize, and maintain energy via her "Be Perfectly YOU!" program. Find out more at: InnerBrillianceCoaching.com

CHAPTER 22

Murmurs of the Inner Voice

José I. Guzmán

*Intuition is soul guidance, appearing naturally in man during
those instants when his mind is calm.*
—— Paramahansa Yogananda

As the plane took off and began to veer away from the Northern coast of Venezuela, I glanced through the window one last time to contemplate the land that my wife, my son, and I were leaving behind. The country we had been born and raised in was submerged in political, social, and economic chaos. I felt a lump in my throat as it was a deeply sad and painful moment —I was leaving behind my family and my mother who was very ill at the time.

Ahead of us was another land full of promise and opportunity, but also of uncertainty as it is for most immigrants. I had accepted a position as a research geoscientist at an oil and gas service company in Houston, Texas, being one of the fortunate ones able to move on after the massive layoffs that shook the Venezuelan national oil company in early 2003. But was it really good fortune that led me to this turning point? Or was there something deeper and more powerful?

Light, Then Darkness

More than a decade before that flight from Venezuela, I had experienced one of the darkest periods in my life. I was working long hours in Caracas and slowly progressing towards a master's degree program in Geological Sciences. But I was painfully unfulfilled and frustrated, even though I had met my lifelong companion and was beginning to be financially stable. I was angry, and my ego—along with other bad habits, such as alcohol use—was pulling me away from the spiritual riches contained in the treasure I had discovered years earlier.

That treasure was Paramahansa Yogananda's *Autobiography of a Yogi*. I was drawn to this book while shopping for a juicer in Colorado, where I was attending college in 1978. The store owner approached me resolutely with a copy and said, "I think you should read this."

As I devoured its pages, I experienced waves of intuitive conviction of Truth. The Inner Voice and Sight within me had been reawakened. Inspired by this book and its profound teachings, I became an adept at yoga and meditation.

Then worldly delusion reclaimed its grip on my soul. I slowly let go of that early inspiration and eventually fell into darkness. My soul fought back as I sought prayerful refuge in local temples and in long, mindful walks. At these times, I felt reassured that *something was going to change*.

The *What If?* Moment

One peaceful and misty Sunday morning, I stood on the balcony of my hillside apartment watching the light traffic on the road that led to and away from Caracas. I would often do this, but this time I was prompted to glance beyond the clouds in the direction of the research campus of the Venezuelan oil and gas company. I knew about this place but had never been there. It had the reputation of being one of the world's prime research institutions, reserved for the industry's best professionals.

On this day, a powerful thought flashed in my mind: *What if I could work there someday?* I sensed fulfillment with this prompting, but my rational mind reminded me that the academic entry requirements were very strict—my intrusive inner saboteur kept telling me to stop dreaming.

A few months after that reverie on my balcony, I was invited to attend a weeklong training for geologists. I connected with old friends and met new ones, but the *What if?* prompting I felt earlier was rekindled during a casual conversation with the leader of the geology department of the research institute, who was also attending the event.

"José, are you aware that we are hiring? We can use someone with your experience," the leader openly shared.

"No, I didn't know," I exclaimed, trying to hide my surprise and excitement. "But I don't meet the strict academic requirements you have."

"That might be changing. Because as I said, we are now valuing experience as well." Her response felt as if a window had suddenly burst open. Then she added, "Let me check with my boss, and I'll get back to you."

The Doors Open

We exchanged our contact information, and a few weeks later, I was invited to apply. After a series of interviews, I was offered a position as a research geologist. The strict academic requirements for entry had just been lifted. Coincidence? On July 20, 1992, I drove through the gates of its beautiful campus and began one of the most rewarding chapters in my life. *The inner murmur I had sensed a year earlier had materialized.*

During the next few years, I unfolded as a scientist, influenced by the best minds I ever had the honor of working with. The work was arduous and challenging but creative, purposeful, and fun. The campus also offered me the opportunity to take long, mindful walks and to find quiet meditation spots after work hours. But I still felt unfulfilled and empty, and I sensed that it was because my ego was winning the battle over my soul—that it was time for me to take firm steps on my spiritual journey. In early 1994, I married the love of my life. A great void in my heart had been filled, but the inner voice kept on murmuring that something else had to change.

One day, I was summoned to an impromptu meeting with the manager of the Department of Geological Sciences. I had no reason to be concerned, although I felt some trepidation when I walked into his office and found that two other leaders were there. After some brief pleasantries, my manager then asked me, "José, how would you feel if we offered you a full scholarship to pursue doctoral studies, conditioned on successfully defending your master's thesis and on securing admissions into a prestigious graduate school in the US?"

My response was of course affirmative, and after months of intense work and preparations, I met both conditions. In August of 1995, we landed in Austin, Texas, where I began a four-year doctoral program at the University of Texas. This was a life-changing experience for my family. It was almost nonstop studying and working, but I managed to keep some balance in my life. Most importantly, I was regaining ground on my spiritual journey and seeing many new professional doors open.

Dark Clouds Ahead

After completion of my doctoral studies, I reactivated my employment at the research institute in Venezuela. My work involved greater responsibilities and pressure, but I would still enjoy my mindful walks around the campus.

At the time, Venezuela was undergoing a deep political upheaval. A destructive agenda was being carried out in the research institute, at first secretly and then openly. What was for many years a fertile ground for great scientific ideas became a political battleground. Similar situations were taking place elsewhere in the country. A major storm was brewing, and I began to seek inner guidance as I felt the need to be prepared in case these events turned ugly.

In 2002, my wife and I became actively involved in peaceful but massive protests that were taking place all over the country. After several months of intimidation and often bloody confrontations, Venezuelan oil industry employees went on an extended strike that climaxed in early 2003 with the firing of over 18,000 workers, including my wife and me. What began as a powerful prompting of the Inner Voice ended in chaos—but such is the cycle of change.

A New Chapter

Fast forward to the flight to Houston—a new chapter in our lives as immigrants was just beginning. For the next twenty years we met numerous challenges, but I experienced steady growth. I regained my footing on the spiritual journey I had begun when I was in college. In late 2020, I retired from my nearly forty-year career as a geoscientist and began my journey as a Life Coach and Transformational Author.

I now understand that I was led to that moment by a series of synchronicities prompted by my Inner Voice, and these occurrences were in response to prayerful moments in times of spiritual need. Many other instances of this inner guidance have taken place since then.

Here is the best part: You, too, have access to this soul-guiding Inner Voice.

Some people call it *conscience* and others a *gut feeling*. It is a manifestation of the intuitive faculty of our souls that can be cultivated at any time by anyone who is receptive.

The spiritual journey may be compared to climbing a steep mountain under the expert guidance of a self-realized master. There are many paths, and the trek is at times steep, but the Guide is at your side in every moment. Occasionally you may turn your head and look at the valley below, distracted by the material wonders you must let go of to make progress towards your own self-realization.

These worldly delusions are so strong that we often fall back down, but your Guide remains on the same spot, patiently waiting for you to ask for help so that you can retrace your steps up the mountain. This is exactly what happened to me.

The Divine is always there, within you and me—patiently listening, waiting, and murmuring.

○

José I. Guzmán, PhD, is a Certified Professional Coach balancing his time in retirement between meditation, service, and coaching professionals and executives to transition mindfully into their next chapter in life—whether it be a new career, active retirement, or uncovering their true purpose. He runs regular workshops on mindful retirement and personal change management.

Visit newshorescoaching.com to access José's exclusive Retirement Preparedness Assessment and to join his private email community for weekly inspiration and tips.

CHAPTER 23

Climbing Out of Codependency

Stephanie Joy Hale

There have been many turning points in my life, several events that
have dramatically shaped the trajectory and outcome of current
circumstances. However, to understand the most important, the most
impactful turning point, you must be familiar with these first two.

When I was fifteen years old, I, like many other girls that age,
met and fell in love with the person I thought was my soul mate.
Unfortunately, this turned out to be a mistake. For the next three
years, I suffered untold physical and mental abuse that left a deep scar.

The second occurrence was in February of 2020, many years after
I walked away from my abuser. I was attending a Brendan Burchard
HPX live event in San Diego, California. I am not normally one to
attend such an event, but I felt compelled to go. My intuition was
correct. By the third day of the event, I could feel my spirit return;
I felt myself becoming hopeful and determined. I absolutely knew I
would finally be able to leave my current job—a job that paid well but
one that I was completely miserable doing. I felt trapped, frustrated,
and often unappreciated. I also struggled with the monotony of it. I

absolutely knew I was meant for bigger and better things; I just didn't know at the time exactly what they were.

As powerful as these moments were in my life; though, they do not compare to the events that took place one day before I sat down to write this chapter—February 14, 2022, to be exact. I discovered that my boyfriend of eight years was having an affair. I always thought of myself as an emotionally strong woman that could handle such an event if it ever occurred. However, I soon found that I overestimated my ability to ignore the heartbreak it caused.

Unfortunately, things between him and me had been going south for quite some time. Our romance was one straight out of a romance novel. We were two high school sweethearts separated by circumstance and rocky childhoods only to be reunited sixteen years later. The relationship began as a whirlwind, both of us caught up in the moment, reliving the old memories, and finally experiencing that first kiss. The adage—*the right person, at the wrong time*—applied. Both of us were exiting long-term relationships, and instead of taking time to breathe and heal, we dived right in.

Our relationship was tested from the beginning. Despite our love, we were bombarded with what seemed like constant loss: the abrupt death of my father; the loss of four pregnancies, two of which could have potentially cost me my own life; and the emergence of poor behavioral and relationship patterns that slowly tore our love apart.

Cheating on someone is never excusable, but I am aware that I played my part. I pushed him away just as much as he pushed me, and we both subjected each other to emotional abuse. You see, I am a codependent person by nature. This leads me into unintentional manipulative behavior to prove I am a good person, a person of worth. I would get angry when my kindness, gifts, and deeds were not reciprocated on the same level. The seed of codependency was planted during my childhood but really bloomed during the time period I was in the dangerously abusive relationship.

He, on the other hand, was highly defensive and prone to shutting me down with his coldness and silent treatment. I felt often as though I was unliked, unseen, and unheard by him, like I was merely tolerated. Because of these dynamics and our inability to express our needs and concerns in a healthy way, he felt that no matter what he did, he would never be good enough for me. So understandably, he left.

These three turning points all play a significant role in both the development, discovery, and eventual recovery from my codependent nature. The first event, long ago and with a different man, is where the codependency really started to set in, take hold, and develop. Many people believe that women will stay in abusive relationships due to low self-esteem. While that may be true in some cases, my situation was different. I believed with all my heart that I could fix this broken man. I thought that all I needed to do was show him how much that I loved him, show him that no matter what he did, I would never leave him. I thought I would heal his heart and we could be together and happy, but I was wrong. One of the first hard lessons I have learned as a codependent is that you cannot fix, save, or heal someone who doesn't want to change. The second lesson is that it wasn't my job to do so in the first place.

In the second event, the amazing Brendan Burchard inspired me to look deep within and question why I do some of the things that I do. *Why did I stay at a job that was not healthy for me for so long? Why did I allow so many people to take advantage of my love, generosity, and kindness? Why do I feel that I need to go above and beyond to prove that I am a good person—someone worthy of love, attention, and friendship?* This turning point led me on a path to discovery, one that would lead to many positive changes.

This third turning point, the loss of my latest relationship was an awakening. It was in this pain that I discovered how my own behavior patterns not only caused some of the stress and negativity in our relationship but also enabled his negative behavior patterns to flourish. While I was critical of both him and the abusive treatment, I also tolerated it.

While this turning point is both heartbreaking and incredibly painful, it has been a lesson well learned. I am thankful I have grown enough as a person to see the good that has come from this. For about a month leading up to my discovery of his infidelity, I knew that something was off. One moment we were trudging along in our relationship, both of us depressed and sullen, and then in what seemed like overnight, he changed. He seemed happier and alive but also more avoidant. Eventually I asked him to leave, knowing that I was setting our relationship up for complete failure, but unable to cope with his blatant disregard for my feelings and infidelity. I was done sitting at home alone.

During this time, I was suffering from severe depression. I felt lost, trapped in the monotony of going through everyday motions. I felt as though I was overwhelmed and constantly busy, yet nothing of substance ever seemed to get done. I had many projects to complete and no desire to finish them. At times, I wished I was no longer a part of this world.

The day I discovered that my love, my best friend, the man that I was supposed to spend the rest of my life with was no longer in this relationship with me, a fire burst within my soul. The pain I felt was so intense that I spent several days trying not to have a panic attack. When the grief subsided, it was replaced with an intense anger that I had never felt before. This anger frightened me. However, over time, the emotions within me began to calm, but that fire was still lit.

Seemingly overnight, I went from not being able to leave my home to someone who couldn't stand being there. I started to go to the gym again. I started to write again. I called up old friends and went out, and I no longer needed to drink four venti lattes to make it to 3 p.m. only to be in bed by 5 p.m. I dropped daily tasks and projects that were no longer serving me.

I was finally reawakened by this breakup, whether despite or due to the devastating heartbreak I felt.

I will no longer tolerate situations that bring me discomfort for the sake of another. I will no longer keep my feelings and opinions hidden in order to avoid upsetting others. I will no longer love bomb individuals to get them to like me or to see my worth. I will no longer put the needs and wants of others above my own because I know that if I love myself first—if I put myself first—then I will be far more capable of loving and caring for others in this world. My heart was broken, yet my life was saved.

Do you find yourself *love bombing* individuals with gifts, praise, and favors to get them to like you or see your worth? If you can answer yes to this, please take a moment to step back and reflect on why this is and what you gain from it. How has it been working for you? If you are in a relationship that brings you discomfort, do not stay for the sake of someone else. Do not keep your feelings and opinions hidden in order to avoid upsetting others. Love yourself first, and your love and care will be multiplied in the world.

Stephanie Joy Hale is a Harvard educated Consultant, Author, and Certified Life and Health Coach who specializes in helping women make difficult transitions and transformations in their lives, specifically women who have experienced and are healing from narcissistic abuse. Currently she offers private coaching and will be hosting her highly anticipated in-person retreats starting in 2023. When Stephanie is not writing or studying for her PhD, you can find her traveling the United States with her pups. For more information, visit: newinsightcoach.com

CHAPTER 24

Shattered Dreams

Kim Han

My eighty-four-year-old husband, Bing, used to go for a walk every single day. One afternoon he told me he was going for a longer walk to see how far he could go. I walked him to the door to say goodbye and watched him walking down the street as he turned to wave. We had been married sixty years, and it was just one of those things that came natural to us whenever one of us left the house.

It was late afternoon when the phone rang. "Kim Han?"

"Yes?"

"It's Queensway Carleton Hospital."

The hospital? Why would they call me?

The first thing the person on the line asked was, "Have the police been to your house?"

The police? "No," a chill gripped my heart. *Why would the police come to our house?*

"Your husband was in an accident."

Oh, my God! I started shaking as images of his bloodied body on the side of the road and the thought that my husband was dead tore through my head like a tornado. I took a deep breath and pulled myself together, hoping that things were not as bad as they sounded. I asked if my husband was okay.

"Your husband was seriously injured, but we are taking care of him." The caller suggested that we come to the hospital right away. I called our son, Jeff, who immediately came to pick me up, and together, we drove to the hospital.

Upon arrival in the emergency department, we were ushered to the cubicle where Bing was lying on a gurney with a brace around his neck and bandages around his head. Medical staff had cleaned him up and dressed him in a hospital gown. His bloodied clothes were piled in a bucket on the floor.

I touched Bing's arm. It was cold. He was semi-conscious and did not react. I was scared but thankful that, at least, he was alive. Nurses kept checking in on him before wheeling him away for X-rays and a CT scan. The result showed broken occipital and collar bones, as well as bleeding in his brain. There was no neurologist at Queensway Carleton, so the ER doctor arranged for an ambulance to rush my husband to the trauma unit of Civic Hospital, a large university hospital in town.

It would be a long night. I kept telling myself: *He'll be all right! He'll be all right. He is strong! He'll be all right.*

We drove to the Civic where doctors and nurses were hovering over Bing. He was attached to all kinds of monitors that were humming and beeping throughout the gloom of the night. The next couple of hours were critical. *Will he make it?* We hung around, worried sick, not knowing what to do. Around 3 a.m., the night nurse told us to go home and rest.

Almost twelve hours had passed since my husband was hit by a car when he stepped off the sidewalk at the entrance to a shopping mall. A car pulling out of the parking lot did not see him, struck him, and hurled him to the ground. That was the moment our lives changed.

After spending a week in the ICU with a TBI (Traumatic Brain Injury), Bing was able to go home. The following weeks were a blur of back-and-forth follow-up visits to the hospital. My husband survived. I was lucky I did not lose him; our kids were lucky they did not lose their father, and Bing was lucky he was in good physical condition for his age. An article about his accident that appeared in the news described him—the victim of the accident—as "a man in his *sixties*." The fact that he was strong and healthy must have sustained him. I wondered if our daughter, Siu-Ling, who passed away exactly two years and two days before Bing's accident, was watching over her dad to spare me from losing him, only two years after having lost her.

The weeks went by in a flurry of appointments with all kinds of therapists. Bing was convinced he was fine and anxious to start doing the things he used to do before the accident, which, in a way, was a good sign. However, for his brain to heal, he needed plenty of rest, sleep, and no screen time. Instead, he continued spending hours in front of the computer like before. His brain injury gradually started to affect his mood and long-and short-term memory, as well as his heart rate, balance, and stability. When his heart rate dropped, he temporarily passed out and collapsed. This is known as *vasovagus syncope*.

Bing tried to be tough and ignored those symptoms. He was anxious to get back behind the wheel, even though I did not feel he should. One day he insisted on driving to his medical appointment. When we came to a stoplight, he suddenly became confused—one major symptom of a TBI. He did not know where we were, even though we had stopped at that same stoplight hundreds of times before.

"Wh-wh-where . . . where are we?" he stammered. "Where do I go now?"

Oh, my! What now? The light changed to green, and we had to move. I tried to keep my cool and told him to turn left. I then guided him to a nearby parking lot, calmed him down, and drove us home.

When I took him to a medical appointment, I told the doctor what happened. The doctor then told Bing that he should not drive anymore as he would pose a danger not only to himself but to others as well.

Bing loved driving. Having his driver's license revoked curbed his independence and bruised his self-worth. It was difficult to accept, and he fell into a deep depression. He became reticent, withdrew into a shell, and lost interest in life and day-to-day living. He used to love classical music, reading, socializing, Skyping, and doing research on his computer. His brain injury washed all that away.

Looking after my husband, house, and home in addition to my work as a librarian and hospital volunteer was overwhelming. I had to give up a job I loved and stop volunteering. It broke my heart when we ended up having to sell our house and to forget our dreams for travel and a peaceful retirement. With a heavy heart, I decided it was time for us to move into a retirement home. We had to dispose of a lifetime of possessions we'd acquired in more than sixty years of our married life. It was horrible!

In the meantime, the doctor prescribed anti-depressants for Bing, but they only made matters worse. He was in a brain fog but was very much aware of his mental and intellectual limitations as a result of his TBI. That was the clincher that made him decide that there was no point in living the way he was.

He shut himself away and started talking about euthanasia. He spent most of his time in bed, sleeping and wishing he was dead. I was exhausted and at my wits' end. There were times when I felt like running away. It made me feel guilty, but I had to do something to take care of myself or I would not be able to take care of him. When he was asleep, I would go on long, solitary walks in the nearby forest to gather my wits and preserve my health and well-being.

I frankly don't know how I managed to keep going, except for the love of my children, friends, and my furry friend, Parker. Being outdoors in nature always has a soothing effect on me. I look, listen, and find gratitude for the little things around me that fill me with wonder—a little ladybird on a blade of grass, reeds waving in the wind, birds calling out to each other and singing in the treetops, or a family of ducks swimming in the pond, leaving ripples in their trail.

According to the *Family Caregivers Alliance,* which offers support and advice to caregivers, taking care of a spouse when one spouse is seriously ill, has dementia, or Alzheimer's, is the most challenging caregiving situation. Bing's case is not that bad, but it still is a challenge.

I must see my glass as half full and give myself a break as I try to find a meaningful way to move forward with the rest of our lives. I decided to slowly wean Bing off his anti-depressants and give him doctor-approved supplements to improve his depressive symptoms and boost his mood. Three years have passed. Bing slowly crawled out of his rabbit hole and started smiling, communicating, and reading books again. I managed to find a kinesiologist who specializes in geriatrics. He offered to help Bing with exercises to regain his strength and balance. I am thankful Jeff was able to persuade his dad to exercise again.

We are learning to accept our new normal and to be thankful for this progress, in spite of our shattered dreams. As you learn to accept your new normal, please take time to care for yourself. See your glass as half full and try to cultivate gratitude as you move forward.

Kim Han, MA, MLIS, is a retired librarian and author of *The Canadian Inuit Dog: Icon of Canada's North* that sold in a dozen different countries. Kim worked in the archives of the International Court of Justice in The Hague, the judicial arm of the United Nations, where she conducted a feasibility study for the automation of the court's antiquated archival system. She lives with her husband and dog in Ottawa, Canada.

CHAPTER 25

The Crowning of Woman

Dr. Tina Hay

It was 4 a.m. Everyone in the house was asleep. Yet, I was behind my desk, inwardly wrestling: *How do I get it all done right? How do I do it all while ensuring everyone feels like a priority?*

Truth be told, I was tapping into every source I knew so that I could pour myself out as a woman, wife, mom, business owner, Soul Doctor, daughter, sister, and friend. The juggling act of meeting the needs, expectations, and demands of others' hearts was weightier than anyone knew. My sincere love for people was greater than my physical ability and time limitations. Yet, there I was, doing my very best to give to the fullest—to everyone but me.

As I sat with my longtime companion, the 4 a.m. hour, life forever changed in a moment as a familiar Presence entered my office. This Presence was the very presence of God. He began to surround me until I felt consumed. I sat motionless and unwilling to move in the Holiness. Deep breaths of reverence were all I could give.

His presence wooed me in, while His unspoken voice echoed within me, "Be still, my daughter. Know that I am God" (Psalm 46:10), as He enveloped me with His unconditional love.

He continued as the imbalance within me steadied, until balance and knowing were achieved. This, my friends, was when His ever-living voice began to speak a union of words in a question I had never heard before. This question, released from His mouth, was left hanging and suspended, all while awaiting my reply. Honestly, I did not want to volunteer the answer. Within my soul, I felt His mystical union of correction and perfect love say, "Tina, do you know what your problem is?"

As only the Eternal could do, I witnessed my own life flash before my eyes as if I was the spectator. His words somehow simultaneously released all of yesterdays—my history, past, and the voices I was carrying within me—words forced upon me without love. I squirmed in my chair as unconditional love allowed my tears to flow while I witnessed my life and each moment of abuse that yesterday held. I knew I needed to surrender each yesterday to answer Him. Finally, I answered His question, "No, I don't. What is my problem?"

His voice spoke again, but this time, it was as if someone had taken a book filled with instant knowing and returned it as a novel onto the shelf of my heart. His voice hugged me as He said, "You have Cinderella Syndrome."

Those four words filled my heart and mind with instant knowing as I relived the folktale of Cinderella. Cinderella is a story about a woman created by design for love, royalty, and success but finds herself caught in a life of obscurity, servanthood, and neglect. I knew exactly what He meant. His words began to hollow out a space within me, evicting everything that was not part of His design for me. This infusion of instant knowledge grabbed hold, and the fit was like that of Cinderella's beautiful glass slipper, but it didn't stop.

Still frozen in the stillness of His Words, as word-infused dialysis filtered out the old and left me with only the new, I was undone. Years of suppressed tears were given permission to cascade down my cheeks and onto my lap as the tyranny of yesterday's control was evicted. My heart flowed forth out of my mouth as I humbly cried, "What now, Lord?"

What I was not prepared for was how this perfect fit of knowing and understanding would create a revolution within me toward my future life, mindset, view of women, ideas of self, and the lifestyle I was trained to live, for I had been trained to live *as one under.*

God's voice continued, "It is time to detox your soul of yesterday. If you allow me to detox your soul, true prosperity and health will follow, and I will never allow your past to torment your future again."

Breathing in the depth of these words, I was reminded of 3 John 1:2, "Beloved, I pray that you would prosper and be in health, even as your soul prospers."

A *yes* response filled me as renewed thinking and proper alignment were offered by my God of Truth. I could clearly see the symbolism of God's words, Cinderella Syndrome, as an identity within me. I had been under those unwilling to allow me to live the life of recognition, success, and royalty I was created to share with the world.

My eyes saw this verse as if for the first time. Everything stopped as I asked myself, *Is it true? Is my thinking the determining factor to my prosperity and health?*

An answer came immediately as Proverbs 23:7 ran through me: "Yes. As a man or woman thinks, so is he or she."

Another nail in the coffin of my yesterdays rang forth.

The hour that followed impregnated me with what today is known as Soul Detox, a wholeness journey brought through me by God. Why? Because I needed it, as do so many others. In my journey, I saw how yesterday's voices from past generations' experiences—the training I was given for who a woman is, what a woman does, how a woman is treated, and the demands a woman is expected to fulfill— were all woven together in the tapestry of my life's identity. Some were good. Others were not. No fault. No blame. I found myself in a simple acceptance of *what is.*

As plumb line questions of truth became altars of transformation, I brought forth the new and understood value found in me: a woman. I asked, "How do I bring this forth into all areas of my life?"

As I examined each area of imbalance I had been given and was living, I did not want a reactionary belief. I sought God's plumb line goal for my life until detox was found. This anchoring truth is a life mission of equal value between men and women. This truth is a motto I decree daily as I invite others into the possibility of what it looks like to live as one: *Honoring man while still celebrating woman.*

My friends, what if it doesn't have to be one or the other? What if it can be both equally? Honor man and celebrate woman. Allow this to ring deep within you. If it does not have the ability to ring, notice the invitation awaiting you—just as it did me. Your health and prosperity are connected to this. I have lived it, and I have experienced thousands of men and women experience it with me.

Was the answer simple? Yes. Has it been easy? No. I have had to intentionally examine every thought and experience I have been given. From religious teachings to cultural traditions, humanity's expectations and practices, a lack of protection, broken legal systems and injustices, my father's lifelong addiction to women, broken and performance-based faith, my personal experiences of abuse, and a life surrounded with male-dominant mindsets—I have stepped into them all. No fault. No blame. It was what it was. But that does not mean it has to be *what is.* I knew I could learn how to love *what is* now as I was given permission to live creating *what is* for the future. So I did.

When I came to this knowing, an illuminated platform was given to me that allowed me to step out from the shadow of man's traditions I had been put under. When I did, I was invited into God's original design for me: Woman—the crowning of man (Proverbs 12:4).

The last thing I ever want to do is feed the historical patterns of abuse—male to female or female to male. No. I want to do this right: *Honoring man while still celebrating woman.*

I want us to do this together. Therefore, I questioned. How do we bring the proper union of man and woman to display the gifts of each one individually?

This is where I saw it: the value of both in perfect union. This is where healing entered my heart like never before. Where there had been misgivings, the truth freed me to see it right as I heard, "A royal crown without a head to rest upon is as incomplete as a king's coronation without the crown."

Can you see it with me? Woman: A priceless, guarded crown meant to be displayed upon the head of royalty. Woman: The royal crowning of man. Man: A king awaiting his coronation and ceremonial crowning moment. Man: The head that the crown, the woman, is supposed to rest upon. Both are equally important, and neither are complete without the other.

This, my friends, is where healing began to flow into my Cinderella Syndrome. I saw that it wasn't just for me. It is for everyone with voices of yesterday. Can we give ourselves permission to create our new *what is?* We all have Cinderella, or Cinder-fella, Syndrome. Yet, we all have the ability to transform our thinking.

I want to invite you to join me in this life journey. Detox your Soul. Become the royal crown or the head the crown rests upon. Be who your Creator designed you to be.

Together, we can honor man while still celebrating woman. Together, we can be one.

The Soul Doctor®, **Dr. Tina Hay,** empowers others to stop questioning life and instead embrace the greatness within. For fifteen years as the Sole-Creator of Soul Detox™ and Co-Founder of Living Life By Design, Dr. Tina has watched miracles emerge as others' yesterdays are redefined and authentic health and success are obtained.

Coaching global leaders in business, government, churches, or homes, Dr. Tina is a master at bringing external results by releasing wholeness within. To learn more about Dr. Tina and Soul Detox, please visit: souldetox.life

CHAPTER 26

The Spirit of Couple Love

Wilfred Holder

After this, the Lord appointed seventy-two other disciples and sent them two
by two ahead of him to every town and place he was about to go.
—Luke 10:1, NIV

In 1972, my company requested me to develop and manage a new branch of their company in Belize City, Belize. I did not know the country, people, or culture. It was indeed a challenge for Kay, me, and our two sons, Christopher aged nine and David aged seven. At the time, we had been married for ten years. It seems, however, that God had a plan for us.

We were both Catholic and attended mass regularly. In January 1976, a parishioner invited us to attend a weekend for married couples. I asked him, "Why us?"

"Well, we see you and your family at church, and we think it would be a good experience. My wife and I would love it if you would accept our invitation."

I said to him, "But we have a good marriage. Not perfect, but compared to many, it's excellent."

He said, "You may not need the weekend, but you deserve it."

We went home, discussed it, and said to each other, *We have nothing to lose*, and made the decision to attend the weekend. After all, it was a good opportunity to get out of the house and spend some quality time with each other.

The first surprise of the weekend was that transportation was provided for us; the second surprise was the venue of the weekend was a farm called Trinidad. This weekend challenged us to look deeply at our relationship. It was an eye opener, causing us to stop and evaluate. I had a real encounter with myself and discovered that I wore the mask of Mr. Strong Man, the great problem solver. What hit me was that I was a sensitive, emotional, and caring person. As I shared my deep love for Kay, I became aware of her deep love for me and her commitment to our faith. We left the weekend with great excitement for our love and marriage.

After the closing mass, we were called by our wonderful teams— the magnificent seven—who consisted of three couples and a priest who had poured out their hearts and souls of their lives to us, and they were all smiling. They had some questions for us: *How did you feel about the weekend? Do you believe God has touched the two of you and your marriage on this weekend?*

We both looked at each other and spoke: "We really had a great weekend. It was hard work and sacrifice. God not only touched us; he embraced us and challenged us to look deeper into our relationship." We were excited about the possibilities of going home to live out God's plan for us.

How do you feel about being one of the team and sharing your couple love?

We replied with one voice: *Yes!* We were all fired up. We were excited. We felt privileged and honored at their invitation to be part of the team. We were then invited to attend a Team Community Meeting. At the end of that meeting, they wanted to know if our answer was still yes and we said, "Yes."

In July 1976, we were sent along with three other couples to do a Deeper Team training weekend in New York, USA. In each presentation, we were called to dig deeper and deeper into our relationship with each other, with God, the church, and the world. As the Teams continued to pour out their life experiences and how they lived out their love for each and God's Plan, tears began streaming down our faces as they challenged us to go out, renew the church, and change the world with our couple love. At our closing mass of our Deeper Weekend, the reading of the Gospel touched us deeply, from Luke 10:1:

> *The Lord appointed seventy-two other disciples and sent them two by two ahead of him to every town and place.*

What was significant to us was that there were seventy-two of us on the weekend.

As the priest and teams laid their hands on us, they said, "Wilfred and Kay, go forth with your couple love, renew our church, and change the world."

At that moment, Kay and I made a commitment to live their words and our mission. We left the weekend with our hosting couple excited and floating on cloud nine.

During our short stay in New York, our hosting couple invited us to share with a group of married couples at their home. As we were saying our goodbyes, the husband of one of the couples held on to us with tears in his eyes. He said, "Wilfred and Kay, I love you. I never thought I would say these words to a black couple, much less hug them. I am a prison warden and work in one of the most dangerous prisons where the majority of the inmates I deal with are black (non-white) criminals, the worst of them. Thank you for sharing your lives. When I go to work tomorrow, I will not be the same. My wife and I thank you for sharing your journey of love here with us and your commitment and dream to change the world."

On the way back to Belize, we were filled with the Dream. Kay and I made a commitment, and at the first opportunity, we packed our bags and headed to Trinidad with our two sons.

From Belize with Love to Trinidad

In 1977, we left Belize with the blessings of our Belizean community to bring the dream of the Marriage Encounter movement to Trinidad, Guyana, and the Caribbean. You may wonder: *Why Trinidad?* The reason was that Kay was born in Trinidad, and I was born in Guyana—therefore, the dream. We arrived in Trinidad to take up residence with our two sons, Christopher and David.

On June 28, 1978, we met His Grace Archbishop Anthony Pantin of the Archdiocese of Trinidad and Tobago at the presbytery of Our Lady of Perpetual Help Parish, San Fernando, where we were able to share our dream of starting Marriage Encounter in the Archdiocese. What started out as a fifteen-minute meeting turned to thirty. After the meeting, he gave us his blessings and said he would get back to us as he was deeply moved by our sharing about marriage and family life. We were excited when we received his letter one week later stating that Marriage Encounter had received his blessings.

The First Marriage Encounter weekend was held on 17–19 November 1978, at Pax Guest House, Mount St. Benedict, Trinidad. There were eleven couples on that first weekend. In 1980, the first movement expanded to Barbados, Guyana, and to the rest of the Caribbean. Today, many of the Caribbean Islands are experiencing these weekends.

These words from our sons Christopher and David will always be in our in our hearts:

"Do you really believe that you can change the world?"

Please do not give up your dream to change the world and to share your love because the world needs people like the both of you.
We love you.
To the greatest mom and dad, we know,
Thank you for all you have done for us.

Our *yes* today is an echo of the first *yes* we said on our wedding day, and we truly believe that God is the center of our lives and that we, Wilfred and Kay, are a living and caring sign of God's Love.

If God has filled your life with love, I hope you, too, will carry that love into the world to bring healing and peace for us all.

○

Wilfred Holder was born in Guyana and is now a citizen of Trinidad and Tobago. He is a lifetime member of the Trinidad and Tobago Association of Insurance and Financial Advisors and MDRT. Wilfred and his wife Kay were awarded the Pope Benedict XVI medal for their work in marriage and family life in Trinidad and the Caribbean. Wilfred is also the author of *One Man's Journey*, available on eBook at Amazon/Kindle. Contact him on WhatsApp at: 1-868-689-4694 or via email: kaishee@gmail.com

CHAPTER 27

When a Heavy Door Closes,
a Lighter One Opens

Stephanie K. Klein

The new president called me into his office. I expected him to con-
gratulate me on our successful rebranding launch the day before.
Instead, he said, "Branding no longer matters."

I felt the ground crumbling beneath me as I struggled to breathe.

I'd experienced that life-threatening punch in my gut several
times, like at age forty-five, when the doctor told me, "You have
cancer, and it's malignant." Now at age fifty-one, I felt this same initial
shock as my identity was shaken to its core.

Two years prior, I'd been recruited as a transformational change
agent—the first Chief Marketing Officer (CMO) in the company's
history with a seat at the management table. I used to pinch myself,
feeling so lucky to be part of a fast-paced, innovative, entrepreneurial
culture where I could speak my mind and run free. I had no idea that
everything would change when we acquired a disruptive startup seven
months before.

Merging two diametrically opposed cultures is tough. I'd convinced our management team and board to rebrand the company under a unified, purposeful vision and identity. I'd passionately led the global team, and we'd succeeded in record time. I was proud and excited to grow our evolved brand yet reported to the new president whose priority was the bottom line.

I'd won in life and my career by figuring out what people wanted and meeting their needs. Now for the first time, I felt at a loss. No matter what I shared, he didn't see the value in my team or my role, and he diminished my scope of responsibility and authority.

In a matter of months, life was unrecognizable. I went from living on an empowered mountaintop to descending into a hole from which I couldn't see my way out. I felt isolated and alone, victimized and angry, and for the first time in decades, experienced debilitating back pain that I couldn't control. Beyond my personal challenges, we navigated layoffs that devastated morale, and our culture became increasingly competitive, stressful, and toxic.

By January 2018, I'd invested months in *making it work* and realized it wasn't. Thankfully, I turned to outside support, asking my former brilliant boss, now mentor and friend, for advice. She said, "Ask for what you want, and show them why it's what you deserve."

I then began my journey to reclaim my power.

Pulitzer Prize-winning writer Alice Walker wisely said, "The most common way people give up their power is by thinking they don't have any." I'd given my power away, but I could reclaim it by writing myself an exit package that would be a win-win for me and the company.

To be effective, I rose above my fear and anger to see the situation from their perspective, so I could clearly lay out the facts and figures of how my position had changed and recommend a win-win solution for restructuring. While my emotions weren't transparent, my values of freedom, growth, and courage gave me the wisdom to write it. I'd hidden my powerful voice under deep layers of armor to survive, but I was ready to speak up for my worth.

What surprised me is that once I decided to exit, my mood and energy shifted immediately, even before the CEO/Chairman who originally hired me said, "We're going to make this right." I had the power to lift myself out of the hole all along, but I needed to first shift from my *victim* mindset to take action.

When I departed in May 2018, the CEO and CHRO advised, "Wait for something worthy of you." My intention was to find a new CMO role with more growth potential and meaning, but first I wanted a Summer of Fun. I desired quality time with my youngest daughter before she left for college in the fall, and I became an empty nester. I'd always regretted not having a free summer since before she started kindergarten, and I could now make her a priority. With plenty of time left for myself, I bought a new bike and rode on the Chicago lakefront and spent time hanging in my new hammock, enjoying the sun's warmth on my face. I loved asking: *What do I really want to do today?* Gradually, I found my equilibrium, joy, and flow again. I rekindled my creativity and reconnected with old friends and colleagues.

Dr. Martin Seligman, the father of modern positive psychology, created the PERMA model for flourishing in life, based on extensive research of what factors foster happiness and thriving (pursuit-of-happiness.org). I was intuitively following this model, beginning with PER, which stand for Positive Emotion, Engagement, and Relationships. And he was right, I felt happier.

If there was a villain during this magical time, it was the pressure I felt to work. I had that fearful insecurity that comes during times of transition: *When will the phone ring again? If I step away, how long will they want me?* As opportunities arose, I realized I was waiting for permission to say *No*, when my therapist reassured me I didn't need it. I learned a valuable lesson: *Yes* lives in the land of *No*. When we say no to something, we are saying yes to something else, even if we don't know yet what will emerge. To really step into my next level authentic self, I had to stop walking in the grooves of my old life so I could see new paths to explore.

In PERMA, the M stands for Meaning. It showed up right on schedule in fall 2018 but very differently than I envisioned. By October, I was interviewing for several CMO positions in mission-driven companies that weren't progressing quickly. I was starting to feel a little behind on my search and decided to de-stress by attending a mindfulness retreat hosted by a friend. I was excited by the promise of beach time, yoga, good food, and connecting with other women. I was less pulled by *mindfulness* but open to exploring. I had no idea how simply becoming more aware would unlock a new door and change the trajectory of my life.

I left realizing what it felt like to connect meaningfully and vulnerably with myself and others. I hadn't been encouraged or rewarded for doing this in my personal or professional life, and the new experience woke me up. I felt energized, emotional, uplifted, seen, and heard. In this space, there were no wrong answers. We listened to Leonard Cohen's "Ring the Bells," and I realized the power in letting go of perfection, as he sang: *There is a crack, a crack in everything. That's how the light gets in.*

I'd never experienced this magic in a group peak experience with such positive energy and radical acceptance. In this safe space, I could embrace my messy, authentic self and connect deeply. I felt love for my fellow women who were bravely facing different life transitions, just like me. I felt love for the teachers and collaborators who had wrestled with finding meaning and now were living more purposeful lives—just as I hoped to do.

I also realized something even more important than what I wanted to *do*; I knew how I wanted to *feel*: light, connected, and fearless in the energy of loving acceptance, joy, and great potential. I wanted to stay far away from the environment of stress and toxicity I'd recently left. Now that I realized what more was possible, I wanted to run toward it! I was ready for the final A in PERMA: Accomplishment. This was a turning point—*I never interviewed for a CMO position again.*

Unknowingly, I'd unlocked a new door that led me toward facing my emotions with vulnerability. In December 2018, I attended a transformational mindful emotional intelligence program called "Search Inside Yourself" (SIY). With more awareness, I realized how stressed I'd been earlier that year and how I couldn't see or think clearly in that hijacked state. I realized I'd cracked the door open to compassion during my cancer recovery, but I had more room to fully open the door to my heart. With greater empathy, I immediately improved my relationships with my eldest daughter and brother. If I could do that in just two days, I wondered: *What more is possible for me and other high achieving leaders?*

I decided to embark on a new journey without knowing where it would lead and write a book on how to do it, as I was doing it myself. I learned to be comfortable with being uncomfortable, which helped me grow more in the last several years than I'd done in the previous thirty.

If you're stuck or in transition, you always have the power to positively change and flourish from your challenges. Begin by facing your fear, uncovering what you need, and deciding what you want. When we shift from a victim mindset, we become more resilient and feel empowered to take action. Each small step forward helps us see with more clarity what comes next. We all face big life disruptions that can feel overwhelming and wrong. Fortunately, what's *wrong* can be our doorway to discovering what's *right*.

Stephanie K. Klein is Founder and CEO of Mindfire Mastery, a coaching consultancy that empowers leaders to balance and optimize performance, relationships, and well-being. Backed by thirty years leadership experience, she serves as an Executive Coach, Leadership and Positive Intelligence Trainer, Educator, Speaker, and Author of upcoming *Waking Up on the Right Side of Wrong*. Stephanie holds an MBA from The University of Chicago Booth School of Business and a BA in Psychology from Duke University. To take one step forward, visit mindfiremastery.com for our free gift, *10 Ways to Wake Up on the Right Side of Wrong*, and to subscribe to our free newsletter.

CHAPTER 28

Am I Gonna Die?

Lori A. Lewis

I opened my eyes to the darkness in the room. *Is it early evening or early morning?* I couldn't tell by the dim light peering through the sheer curtains in the room. I was disoriented and wondered where I was.

My left arm was tethered by a cuff, and an IV was in my right arm. I looked up to see a dark figure tending to the cuff. She looked like an angel, and without thought, I heard myself ask in a voice that sounded unfamiliar, "Am I gonna die?"

Without speaking, she took my hands and pushed my fingers up into a praying position. Then, she covered my hands with hers and began to pray over me. Years of bad decisions began to fall from my eyes. Later that night, as I lay in that hospital alone and afraid, I realized how my life choices had led me there and that I wanted to live. I also knew that this night was the greatest turning point in my life.

***

Millions of Americans are diagnosed with illnesses each year related to the choices they make every day like smoking, drinking, and eating a poor diet. Here is my story, one of a lifetime of food addiction and then later in life, addiction to alcohol.

Twenty years earlier, I was an ER on-call social worker. My weight had shot up to 267 pounds. I was in my thirties at that time, a single mother of a seven-year-old son. I kept hearing about these nurses who were getting this weight loss surgery and losing an enormous amount of weight. Yo-yo dieting had afflicted me my whole life, so the chance of getting to normal weight was irresistible, and I had gastric bypass surgery in 2001.

I was told at the time that I might not want to drink alcohol, but since it had never been a problem before, it really didn't register to ask why. The surgery was successful, and for the first time in my adult life, I was at a normal weight. You see, I was always the girl with *the pretty face*—the kind of thing someone says to you when what they really mean is that the rest of you is too fat. My newfound attention from men was confusing and overwhelming. I was a thirty-six-year-old woman, but my emotional and maturity skills around men were that of a sixteen-year-old girl. Growing up in the '70s and '80s, curvy and overweight girls didn't get asked out that often. So, I didn't have much experience with this type of attention.

Shortly after the weight loss, I got a job in pharmaceutical sales, making twice as much as I did as a social worker. After a layoff in 2002, I went into medical sales in the hearing aid business. I now was making six figures. As a single mom, I thought I would never be able to buy a house, send my son to college, or even be able to retire. So, I left my love of helping others and began to *chase money*. Sales came easily to me, and I was successful.

In 2006, I decided to start my own audiology practice. I knew nothing about business, but I was tired of traveling. I also believed in myself and my ability to learn. I grew my company into one of the biggest and most successful independently owned practices in the country. However, I was miserable. Anyone who owns a business knows there is no real turning it off. I began a ritual of drinking a glass of wine at night. When the recession in 2008 began, I had way too much overhead, and I needed to make some difficult business decisions. My company survived; however, it took a huge toll on me.

My marriage at the time did not survive, and I found myself twice divorced. That one glass a night turned into three, and as time passed, it became even more. Food had not been a viable option to self-soothe since the surgery, so alcohol became the crutch that I believed was the only way I could turn it all *off* at night. The truth of the matter is that I had no real coping skills.

I grew up in a family with a mentally ill and absent mother and an alcoholic and abusive stepfather. Coping skills were just not high on their priority list to teach us kids. I coped through life by being driven, first academically and then professionally. I found that if I stayed busy, then I didn't have to ponder such silly questions or thoughts about how I was coping. To me, my feelings were seemingly unimportant, and my behavior was greatly ignored.

I sold the practice in 2019 and pursued my passion to become a certified professional coach. Typical of me, I couldn't work with just one certification program; I was working on two at the same time. It was like working and going to graduate school, both full time. I had been sober for months, but still had a few slips. I was excited to start the new chapter in my life.

The next summer, I began to feel increasingly weaker and couldn't attend family get-togethers. I eventually wound up in the Emergency Room. Years of fatty foods and too much alcohol had damaged my liver with disease. Gastric bypass surgery reroutes the surgically reduced, egg-sized stomach into the small intestines so blood alcohol levels peak much higher than before the surgery. I didn't realize that even though a person may drink as much as before surgery, the alcohol will be processed faster and the effects will be greater. Liver damage may occur much quicker for these persons than for those without the bypass.

So, I lay in a hospital bed, not knowing if I would survive. The one thing I knew about myself is my ability to adapt and change when needed. Boy, I needed to. My very life and all I had worked for were in jeopardy. When I got out of the hospital, I decided to change my life. I needed to see those future grandkids.

The first thing I did was take a hard look at my coping skills. As I had completed my certifications, I could see how I lacked the ability to handle my thoughts, feelings, and behaviors. I hired a therapist who specialized in working with childhood trauma. I also attended recovery groups.

The second thing I did was learn to set boundaries with others as well as myself. I cut out the negative and drama-laden people in my life. I surrounded myself with positive and like-minded people, especially those in my coaching community. I stopped watching so much news; I decided I would no longer live my life by other people's playbooks. Additionally, I stopped trying to please everyone at the expense of myself.

The third thing I did was practice better self-care—not just traditional external care (like getting my nails done or getting a massage) but also internal self-care. I listened to the way I talked to myself.

Do you know that internal voice that tells you that you are not good enough, pretty enough, or smart enough? *Enough!*

I began offering myself grace, the kind of grace I would offer my best friend. I learned to be my own best friend. I learned to say no to what I didn't want to do and yes to more playtime.

In America, we hold our eighty-hour workweeks up like a badge of honor. At one time, I was one of those people. I learned how to incorporate some playful things, like riding my bike, taking a hike, and dancing to '80s music in my living room. A lifelong worrier, I now do something I have never done before. In the morning, I write down my list of intentions for the day. It includes one household chore, a list of work tasks, and one thing I will do for play. When the list is completed, I am done for the day. If a thought or a worry comes into my head, I tell myself, *not today*. If it is not on the list, I can address it tomorrow. I used to become so overwhelmed that I would do nothing. This practice alone has significantly reduced my stress levels.

As Bonnie Mohr says, "Life is not a race, but indeed a journey." Well, I'm still on that journey. I'm far from perfect with all these new practices. However, I am committed to trying to be the best version of myself. My diagnosis was scary, but the gifts I received from it are invaluable. Today, I maintain a healthy weight, I'm sober, I get to help others on their path, and I am incredibly grateful for all of these new and better ways to create a life that works for me.

If you are facing a difficult medical diagnosis, I know it can seem overwhelming and may seem an abrupt end to your life as you once knew it. Take a deep breath; it most likely is not exactly what you are thinking. Check in with your feelings. Behave in a way that brings the best care for you. Be your own advocate. Know that you are not alone. We all face demons at one time in our lives. Be courageous and mighty. All experiences are opportunities for growth. You, too, can find a way to create a life that works for you.

○

Lori A. Lewis, MSW, is an Educator, Advocate, Social Worker, professional Certified Coach, and lifelong helper. She is a successful entrepreneur, having built a highly successful audiology practice for the hearing impaired. She now is the CEO of Lori A. Lewis Coaching, LLC, dedicated to helping other female entrepreneurs and executives navigate the challenges of addictions. She is passionate about educating and helping weight loss surgery survivors learn about the dangers of cross-addiction. For more information about this author, visit: lorialewiscoaching.com

CHAPTER 29

Discovering My Conscious Heart

Chequita McCullough

It was days before I was about to turn fifty, and my life was unraveling around me. I was in loveless marriage; the job I loved was coming to an end; I was in debt, living paycheck to paycheck; and I was overweight again.

This was not the first time I had been down this road. It seemed every decade I found myself at the exact same place. *Why do I keep repeating this same cycle?* My life felt like a rollercoaster ride, but it was the same rollercoaster, the same difficulties with the same twist, all leading to the same place at the end of the ride—me feeling broken mentally, spiritually, and physically. I heard a saying uttered by older people: *Your life gets better in your fifties. You will be smarter and wiser*, they all said. Really?! From where I was standing at forty-nine, I could not see *better* on my path. I only saw my path with a pattern of sameness that could not be changed or broken. At this point, I was not sure I wanted to turn fifty. If it was going to be an unfulfilling life, what was the point?

Then I remembered I had once read a book about growing older and aging well. This book shared stories of people who had overcome tremendous odds or poor choices they had made in their twenties, thirties, and forties and somehow got it together after turning fifty to live fulfilling, and in most cases, extremely successful lives. I remember reading this book in my early forties and being excited to become smarter and wiser when I entered my fifties.

All I could see was that my life was a series of failures. I had become a statistic, a person created with lots of potential and promise who missed those opportunities because of poor choices. I had broken my own heart. When I looked back over my life, I had no one to blame but myself. I realized somewhere long ago, I had given up on myself. It did not matter what my friends, family, and coworkers thought of me—which was all loving—I did not believe I deserved their love, their friendships, or their support because I was not worthy.

When we do not feel worthy, we create a lonely space that allows us to isolate, to reject good things, and to refuse to grow or develop within ourselves. This, in turn, leaves us feeling desolate, empty, and barren of feelings on the inside, operating from a shell of the person we are meant to be. All I knew during these last few days before my birthday was that I did not want to feel like this anymore. After three decades of pretending to be happy, I wanted to be happy with myself and my life. What I needed to do was discover the missing link in my life. *What was keeping me stuck on the rollercoaster of emotional brokenness and emptiness?*

I believe God is real and that He listens to my prayers. However, the one thing that I had not done through my rollercoaster life was constantly stay connected to God. My adult life had been filled with what I wanted to do with no connection to the outcome—good or bad. This pattern often led me into the proverbial pickle, and then I would pray for God to rescue me out of the mess I'd created. I knew I was not living a Christian-centered life, but I thought I knew better than God.

So, in one of my prayer sessions during this time, I prayed for God help me make the second part of my life far exceed the experience of the first part of my life. I asked him to help me live my life for the purpose He created for me. Then I committed myself to Him fully and asked that He reshape, mold, and clean me up into His image. I wanted to study Him deeply, so I could learn and understand just how powerful and magnificent I understood Him to be—beyond just reading the Bible.

I asked Him to reshape me into a person I could not recognize when I looked in the mirror. I asked Him to fix my broken heart. Then I wrote this statement and posted on my bathroom mirror for a year: *The second half of my life is going to be better than the first half.* I did not know how it was going to change, but I was determined. I knew I had to do things differently to reach a new result. I repeated this declarative statement until I believed it, not with my head but with my heart.

My birthday finally arrived, and I decided I wanted to do something different. I called a friend to see if I could spend time with his mother. She had recently been diagnosed with breast cancer for the second time. I had not seen nor spoken to her in thirty years. I would visit her in the coastal city of Monterey, California, where I grew up, so I was excited to drive down and see the ocean as it has always brought me peace and serenity.

As I started the drive, it was a beautiful sunny day in San Jose, California. The sky was so blue on this cool February morning. As I drove through the fields of Gilroy, I could smell the familiar garlicky air as the wheels of my car hummed against the highway. As my SUV continued the journey, my excitement and nervous energy continued to grow. I asked myself: *What wisdom am I going to learn from this meeting? What life lessons will she teach me that I do not already know?* As I rounded the curve to connect to the final highway before reaching my designation, I saw the mighty Pacific Ocean churning against the shoreline. In that moment, I knew I was going to receive some type of healing for my soul that day.

I finally made it to her house, and when I arrived, she was waiting for me at the driveway where she embraced me with this enormous hug of love. It was as if God was hugging me through her. Even though it was my birthday, I had decided I wanted to shower her with gifts, so I brought bags and bags of things for her to open on my birthday. Because of chemotherapy, she could not enjoy most foods as she could not taste them, but she could taste potato chips. We ate potato chips and drink herbal tea while we sat at her kitchen table for the entire day until sunset, talking and laughing about womanhood, marriage, children, and life. It was truly an amazing day. This day was a turning point moment that changed my life forever because this is the day I discovered my conscious heart.

There were so many lessons God showed me through her as we sat at that table on my fiftieth birthday. He showed me that receiving healing and forgiveness for our past mistakes heals our hearts. Mistakes will happen, but they are opportunities to gain experience and develop our character as individuals.

When we develop our character, we become self-assured and confident in what we do and speak. We learn that we are resilient, courageous, and most importantly, we are survivors of life's rollercoaster moments. Our mistakes are also steppingstones to help others, creating familiarity so others can see how we overcame obstacles and gained success.

He showed me humor in that we cannot take things too seriously because every circumstance will be over in a blink of an eye. If we focus on our painful failures, we will never see or experience the joy that life brings. We always hear laughter is medicine for the soul. When we laugh, our vibrational energy rises, bringing us to a new heightened awareness; from there, we can feel optimism and see better things ahead while our heart beats with hope.

Lastly, He showed me unconditional love and what it looks like coming from a person whose body was battling cancer. She showered me with love, wisdom, and knowledge that led me down a new path of self-love and discovery. Through this encounter, God showed me how He loves all of us whether we believe in Him or not. He changed me into someone I do not recognize. When I look in the mirror, I see a face full of joy, happiness, hope, and love, ready to help transform the world. God taught me that He created this Earth for us to love one another and live in community, helping each other along the way.

Do you see the same old patterns in your life that have not led to happiness? Perhaps, you need to act and better your own life instead of waiting for someone else to do it for you. I invite you to take your turning point moments, which are stepping-stones of wisdom on your life journey, and use them to change not only yourself but the world.

As a newly published Author, Speaker, Moderator, Master Coach, and Leadership expert, **Chequita McCullough** teaches people how to move beyond their self-created limitations by coaching them to empowerment by shifting their mindsets, emotions, and actions beyond limitations. Featured in *Forbes Magazine* as a "One of Five Women Thriving in a Male Dominated Industry," Chequita lives in San Jose, California, where she leads people to live full, authentic lives. Visit Chequita at: chequitamccullough.com

CHAPTER 30

Hashtag#!

Dr. Angela Mendoza

It was happening—Thailand 2018.

Brokenhearted, I embarked on my first international trip. I had innumerable fears of catching malaria, being kidnapped, or being completely lost in a place where English wasn't the dominant language. I had been waiting my whole life to find the ultimate traveling companion, and at this point, I was exhausted of waiting for Mr. Right. I realized that if I had a dream, I could not rely on others to make it happen. I needed to take the first leap and trust the Universe's guidance. I mustered all of my courage and dove headfirst into pursuing my dream with a sink-or-swim mentality.

I was pleasantly surprised when my journey began on a tour in which the majority of the patrons were young women between eighteen and twenty-four years of age. I quickly noted I was the oldest female: standing 5' 4", 122 lbs., and thirty years of age. These adventurous women watered a seed inside of me that inspired me to continue to be daring with my travels, even if that meant alone.

I have assigned hash-tags to years of my life since 2016. In that year, I was brutally honest with myself and titled it #Keepinitreal2018!

The journey continued on to Koh Panghan at Wonderland Healing Center where I met even more remarkable women and encountered an unforgettable restorative atmosphere. Wonderland provided a place where visitors could thrive on a vegan diet, participate in therapeutic yoga, unwind the mind with daily meditation, and meet a community of like-minded souls. Here, I met a brilliant entrepreneur gifted with strategic insight, an enthusiastic cancer survivor running her own non-profit holistic festival in the UK, and a skilled accountant with a passion for providing quality organic farming in Australia, to name a few.

We all shared a longing for connectedness and a genuine desire to help better humanity through our gifts, compassionate natures, and open hearts. We wanted to bring more joy and love into the world by offering our own unique skillsets flavored with the spices of life experience.

There was an opportunity for each person to grow because of the sanctuary we created to let go of pain, confront fear, and express frustrations of the past, present, and future. This sacred place was possible because of our non-judgmental presence and our respectful choice to provide advice from an altruistic place only when requested. Through this, we were able to give each other things money couldn't buy—joy through gratitude, courage to follow our intuition, love to share with others, peace through presence, and hope in a better future through being the best versions of ourselves.

The courage that was ignited in 2018 after taking that first dive into solo-traveling encouraged me to remain curious and self-reliant and to dream bigger than I ever dared. It also left me with more questions on how to better serve people in an atmosphere similar to what I found in Thailand.

As a doctor of physical therapy, I was trained to promote healing and functionality by maximizing the efficiency and the use of the musculoskeletal system in conjunction with *osteokinematics* and appropriate body mechanics. However, I knew that there is much more to a person than their physical body; they also have an emotional and mental body as well. These other bodies are equally important, if not more so.

The experiences of Thailand served to model a way I could connect more deeply with my patients by providing them a non-judgmental sanctuary to share their struggles, connect them to a community, and empower them with current knowledge. In this sanctuary, I found that many of them were wrestling with emotional and mental disorders.

Thailand was not the first time in my life I felt emotionally unsettled. I struggled with depression during my teenage years, and I clung to the cliché, *Everything happens for a reason,* for comfort. I carried those words a step further in the hope that I could learn how to help myself in order to help others who suffered similarly. Being heard is a good start, but it is important to take the next step to make sure you get the help that you need. There is no shame in seeking assistance if you are physically injured, and there should be no shame in needing help if your mental and emotional bodies are imbalanced.

A lesson I learned from these experiences is that the art of healing requires you to dig deeper than your skin and bones into the mental and emotional realms. It requires you to take a closer look at what you're thinking and feeling and then to understand that you are neither of those things. Emotions are fleeting, and thoughts don't define who you are—your actions and the way you live your life do. It is only by turning on the light of awareness that you can find the door out of your suffering. If you know the problem, you are halfway to the solution.

I may have started my transformative trip to Thailand disheveled and heartbroken, but I ended that time wanting to share my experience with everyone—even to this day. A seed was planted in me that grew into a purpose to empower the next generation to commit to self-love through self-care.

Diet and exercise are important to care for your physical body, but you need to continue to nourish your mind and soul as well. I continued with this open heart and mind set into the following year with this hashtag: #WildandFree2019! In the summers of 2018 and 2019, I indulged in sweat lodges, vibed with sound healing workshops, and participated in different yoga and meditation practices. I also reflected on my Latin American ancestry and completed the Salkantay trek to Machu Picchu, participated in a ten-day Vipassana retreat, backpacked through Europe for two months, reunited with my dear friend Sophie at the Holistic Healing Festival in the UK that she hosted, backpacked in Michigan with my soul sister Kat, and enjoyed the Conscious San Jose Festival in my new hometown. These experiences continued to fuel me with further ideas and grander dreams to share with the world.

Then COVID 2019 reared its head around the corner into 2020 and never left. The pandemic took us all by storm. Neither you nor I could possibly guess the length of this pandemic or the effects of it on our physical, mental, spiritual, emotional, and social well-being. It was clear to me that what started as a hope of sharing information on self-care, transformed into a necessity to get this information out as soon as possible. Thus 2020 became: #Thevision2020!

During 2020, I began to explore and learn more about the impact of nutrition on preventing leading causes of death, improving emotional well-being, and increasing immunity. I also learned about the impact of lifestyle choices in the healing process. I became certified as a Holistic Nutritionist and Lifestyle Medicine professional.

It was time to put these pieces together and roll into: #Makingthedream2021! I collaborated with my manager and other colleagues to launch two whole food plant-based diet classes at the facility where I worked. I also began incorporating more thorough assessments of patients' mental and emotional statuses by evaluating their stress levels and giving them the time they needed to be heard. I began writing a book that addresses how to stay balanced during times of flux and uncertainty and the benefits of self-love through self-care.

I want to inspire you to take the first leap in trying to heal yourself in order to better serve your soul. I believe you are here for a purpose and only you can find that purpose.

Taking chances to pursue your dreams in ways you feel safe is important, but it can be difficult to find this purpose or serve your soul when you are imbalanced. It is not impossible; if you continue to seek, you will continue to find. Being honest, patient, and encouraging to yourself are great ways to get started.

You are a living, breathing entity and worth the time and energy required to take care of yourself. One of the greatest gifts you cultivate with awareness is understanding yourself and how you are intimately connected with everything and everyone around you.

My mother always told me, "You are your best doctor."

Your body is amazing, and it has the power to repair itself more than you can believe. You know yourself best. I believe she is right, and I preach it to all of my patients. I tell them, "I am a guide, but your body is the boss." Your way of healing may be different than someone else's, and that is okay.

Life is a journey, and we all have the same destination. However, by building a better relationship with your lifelong partner—yourself—it will be a smoother ride. A destination is only as good as the company. There is no time better spent than getting to know yourself and what you need to live your best life.

I endeavor to live my happiest and healthiest life through physical, emotional, mental, and spiritual well-being with a deep commitment to serve the community I live in. This choice has led me to my current hashtag: #LivingtheLife2022!

Forthcoming author of the book, *Balanced: Five Pillars*, **Dr. Angela Mendoza** is a Physical Therapist, Holistic Nutritionist, and Lifestyle Medicine Professional. She is a social vegetarian/in-home vegan, minimalist, triathlete, and yogi. She leads an active lifestyle in her community. Angela practices what she preaches and is involved in speaking at local schools, facilitating multiple whole food plant-based classes, and is a mindfulness advocate. Check her website for updates on her book and other tips at: mytribehealing.com

CHAPTER 31

Jump!

Phyllis McLaughlin Nauman

Sometimes death approaches disguised as a young woman driving a 3800-pound Chevy Impala—an unexpected and rude intrusion as that night was a night to play. Gifted with tickets, my friend and I headed to Angelle Hall. I needed the healing sounds of live music to clear me after a rough October week. The fourteenth anniversary of my older sister's death overlapped the three days spent with my younger sister, who struggled with the end stages of Lewy body dementia (LBD). I had spent the last two nights awake at the hospital bedside of a family member who had triumphed and survived cancer surgery. My body, mind, and spirit felt fatigued by these events. Everything in me called to spend time in both prayer and play as a way to regather my own healing energy.

My date, skilled at injecting humor medicine to brighten moods, commented about needing to howl at the beautiful, almost full moon. *Let's celebrate life!* I was playing with the sound of the words, *a waxing gibbous moon,* trying to decide whether—after the concert—to draft a poem first or to look up the symbolism of this celestial sign. Dee and

I moved hurriedly down the sidewalk on Saint Mary Blvd. Concert goers surrounded us as we arrived at the corner and approached the cross walk. Time, according to the signal light, was ticking down but there was no hand saying *halt*.

With the practice of a lifetime crossing city streets, I looked, left, then right, then left again—no traffic. Feeling safely illuminated by the moon and a huge streetlight, we stepped off the curb. There were three people ahead in the crosswalk, then my friend and I, and two women followed. I took a long, deep breath and glanced up at the moon.

Jolted, I heard my friend yell, "Watch! You are about to hit two of us!"

What I saw next is still seared in my brain: the grille of a large car was just inches from my body. People say that when you are facing death your life flashes before your eyes. Instead, my brain and being rushed fast forward. Like a dark movie, I saw myself dragged under the car, and then I saw myself in surgery, followed by intensive care on life support with my head and body swathed in bandages. The final scene revealed that I was in rehab, barely functional. It was like a bizarre dream. I could, feel, smell, and taste each of those experiences: the smell of the undercarriage, the heat of the engine, my consciousness hovering over my body as I was in surgery, the intensive-care unit, and rehab.

What if in a microsecond, a miracle moment, a time marked as fast as hummingbird wings or a newborn's heartbeat, you can change your life?

There was not even time for the words to come out of my mouth. I thought: *no!* In the next moment, love touched me from the other side of the veil. In that millisecond, I felt completely supported by angels, guides, and benevolent ancestors. I believed there were no limits to what was possible, and I did not have to accept the fate that looked inevitable. I said *yes!* to living no matter the odds.

I heard my mother's heaven-sourced voice say, "Jump!"

Immediately, I went into Taiji defend-and-gather energy pose: my left arm extended with palm up, right arm close to my body, palm out and shielding my face. With Ninja like presence, I jumped high and pulled myself into a ball of energy. Women screamed loudly around me, and I heard the thump of my body as it contacted the hood of the car. My mind still raced and allowed me to see what was happening as though in slow motion. All the weight of my body was balanced on my left hand and arm, like some wild break dancer.

Before my face could crash into the windshield, I saw the driver, a girl with her face frozen like the painting, *The Scream*. My face mirrored hers! Suddenly, the driver hit the brakes, and I was flying. Per witnesses, I did a curled, triple summersault in the air and landed in the opposite traffic lane on my hands and knees. A flood of thoughts zinged through my brain: *Oh my God! What just happened? Get out of the street before another car hits you. Thank you, Momma! I'm so glad I didn't have time to change out of my jeans. I am still alive; I am alive, conscious, and breathing. I am alive! How did we do that?*

A frisson passed through me like hot chills, and I shook myself to focus. My body felt leaden, and I talked myself into standing up. As soon as I lifted my left hand, my arm torqued, and it felt like my curled hand was glued to my chest. *Still, I must rise.* Pushing on my right hand and opposite knee, I was able to flex my right leg and then pull myself to standing position.

I felt another rush of adrenaline, and I uncharacteristically wanted to run. My friend appeared at my side, and I frantically babbled, "Let's go. Come on, let's run. Let's run; we can make the concert in time. Let's run!"

Wisely, he put his arm around my shoulder to support me as I took my first steps. Quietly he said," Sweetie, you were just hit by a car; come sit down for a minute while we sort this out."

Miracles, moments, the prophetic dreams of a thirteen-year-old, angels, choices, love, Taiji, my momma's voice—how did the Universe weave all that together so that I am here to share this with you? I do not have all the answers, but I do have a deeper understanding of the path.

Part of the miracle is that when I heard my mother say, "Jump!" I didn't say, "But I'm sixty-three, I can't jump that high." Nor did I say, "Jump? Do I have to? How high?" Another response could have been, "Uhm, can I read another chapter first? I am at the good part." For the loving, persistent guidance of family, friends, and teachers who have helped be awake and to live in the present moment, I am deeply grateful.

What are my big lessons in this Jump?

Choice: Computers rapidly make only two choices. Sometimes the world wants us to believe we have only two choices (good or bad), but we are more than artificial intelligence. When you choose to say, *no!* to something that does not feel right to you, you do not have to have the answer to what *yes!* will look like. Trust yourself and your inner knowing. We have a right to choose as we were born into a freewill universe. Not everything is predestined. As BE-ings of divine light, we are not locked into the inevitability of fate. We can rewrite our life scripts as we co-create our lives when connected to a Divine flow of love. Love connects us to the *yes!* of Life. You are allowed to change your mind and make choices in every present moment.

I'm-possible: Like you, I am a spirit wandering this Earth in a body suit that is often at odds with my potential. In my dreams, spirit journeys, and meditations, I dance and fly freely. There are no limits. Our consciousness accepts these images as part of our reality. At age forty-three, I started Taiji, seated in a chair in a class of women who were sixty to eighty years old. Something like magic occurred as the class reminded me of what my mother had taught me about the intention that every breath be a prayer, a Divine connection. In the lineage of Professor and Master Taiji instructor, Yang Yang, I participated in his weekend submersion. He told me, "You've got this. Do some every day, and you will be well." I encourage you, dear one, to pursue gentle activities that will strengthen you and give you freedom to move and breathe.

Precognitive dream: While crossing the street on a college campus, I am struck by a car. Thrown to the sidewalk, I curl into a ball crying, "I do not want to die alone." Mother Mary in a modern blue dress came and held me in her arms as I stopped breathing. Angels appeared on my left and right sides putting their wings around my shoulders, and we moved upwards into a beam of light. Suddenly, we floated through a crystal corridor. Angelic beings escorted me into a room with a huge, bright silver and gold mirror.

I asked, "Am I in Heaven?"

They replied, "No, not yet."

When you can look in the mirror and love everything you see, then you will be in heaven. I felt huge love. Closing my eyes, I spiraled down into my bed and woke. To learn how to have heaven on Earth and feel angelic support was life-changing then and gave me my life fifty years later.

Spiritual meaning of the waxing gibbous moon: I learned that October is the Pisces moon. Like the fish, we swim in a flow of opportunities that exceed our usual understanding of time / space limits. Its light casts meaning through symbols and images and informs our consciousness.

What if you can change your life in the field of all possibilities in a moment? This is the gift of dwelling in the present moment, loosening the restrictions of a ticking clock. Take a deep breath, sigh, then smile. You can choose a place where heaven is at hand and miracles lovingly manifest.

Phyllis Mclaughlin Nauman, RN, BA, is a mystic, writer, dancer, and artist who has used her Angelic connection in her Holistic wholeness practice. Light language, ancestral communications, Reiki, IET, and Shamanic sound healing are her tools for sharing the Divine love energy, *Angel Fire*. In October of her thirteenth year, she had a prophetic death dream that revisited in October fifty years later and provided her miraculous *Turning Point Moment*. Email: PhyllisMNauman@VerbalCollage.com. Subject line: Angel Fire Connections or Verbal Collage

CHAPTER 32

D. I. Y. ZEN and The Art of Happiness, Kindness, Blessings, and Gratitude

Gary Nobuo Niki

In almost sixty years, there have been so many powerful turning point moments that occurred in my life thanks to my mom and dad. They raised me to understand the process and concept of D.I.Y. Zen and the art of happiness, kindness, blessings, and gratitude.

As I was growing up, no matter what happened to my mom and dad, they lived their lives demonstrating how Do-It-Yourself (D.I.Y.) Zen would be important to me and that being Zen started from the inside of us, especially when it came to living the art of happiness, kindness, blessings, and gratitude.

My dad, Carl Nobuo Niki, was born in 1915—half Japanese (dad), half Mexican (mom)—grew up throughout the 1929 stock market crash, Great Depression, and soup kitchen era. During World War II, he was arrested for being Japanese. He served six months in a Japanese internment camp, then raised his hand, swore in as a United States Merchant Marine, and served out the rest of the war on ships overseas.

My mom, Kay Keiko Mataga, was born in 1931. Being full Japanese, she and her entire family were arrested and sent to the Japanese internment camps in Jerome, Arkansas and Sacaton, Arizona during WWII.

Even though my dad and mom lost everything—including their freedom—for just being Japanese, they learned to live their lives in D.I.Y. Zen while they practiced the art of happiness, kindness, blessings, and gratitude every day, no matter what occurred. They passed on the practice and concept to me, and I now share it with you.

I grew up in Paradise Valley, Arizona. In 1965, it was desert with dirt roads, cactus, and tumble weeds, in the middle of nowhere just like in the black-and-white cowboy movies I watched as a kid. When I would say I was bored, miserable, upset, or lonely, my mom would say, *Go play with your little sister* or *Go outside and make your own fun.* She would tell me that I must be happy on my own, by myself, making my own happiness when nobody was around. *You can be happy and joyful while playing, using your imagination to make and do things for yourself.*

I have to admit as I'm writing this in early 2022, I am still grieving the death of my mom in December 2021. As I'm thinking about all of the wisdom, insights, guidance, and kindness that I received from my mom and dad, I am so grateful, happy, and blessed that I had my mom for as long as I did here on Earth School.

In my book, *D.I.Y. ZEN and The Art of Gentle Emotional Transformation,* I wrote a lot about my dad. Here, I'm including some of my mom's wisdom and guidance too.

My mom would become Mrs. Kay Niki. She and my dad were two of the best examples of *good humans* who lived and demonstrated happiness, kindness, blessings, and gratitude every single day no matter what happened to them. During my lifetime, there were so many times I witnessed these qualities in my mom and dad.

Our house was hit by an F-2 level Tornado June 21, 1972. It took three quarters of our house with us inside of it; we lost almost everything. After the storm, the first thing my dad and mom said was, "Thank God! How fortunate and grateful we are that all of our family, cats, dogs, guinea pigs, and parrot survived uninjured. No matter what we lost, we are alive and blessed."

On June 3, 1983, my dad had a heart attack and died suddenly at only sixty-seven years old. It was devastating for me. At twenty-one years old, I was attempting to be strong for the family, and my mom said, "Son, you have to be grateful we had Dad as long as we did and the two of you were best friends. You have so many happy memories and blessings from him that you will carry with you throughout your life, along with his wisdom, kindness, and love for us. I miss him too. For over twenty-seven years he was my best friend, the love of my life, and he sure loved all of us. I'm so grateful, even though I'm brokenhearted. I know we will come through stronger because of your dad's love, kindness, and huge happy smile that he shared every day with us and the world."

A few years later my mom developed breast cancer, had a radical mastectomy, and was amazingly happy, grateful, blessed, and Zen throughout her recovery.

As I think of her, I am crying so hard that my notebook is getting wet. I'm processing the loss of my mom by putting my fingers on my forehead and clearing out the pain of her death. I have recovered and am now back to writing.

At this moment, I feel so happy, blessed, and grateful that even though it took me twenty-two years to get my first book published, I was able to sign and share it with my mom before she died. Mom was in assisted living for memory issues, and at eighty-nine years old she was not able to read my book. However, she loved the pictures, and her kind caregivers would read my book to her. They told me that all of sudden my mom would light up, get very talky, laugh, and tell them all about a story I'd shared in the book. I'm grateful that some things in my book would spark her memory and that she was able to tell her story too.

When it came to kindness, my mom and dad were the best, and even though my mom was quiet and reserved—the exact opposite of my dad who was hugely known and loved, friendly, gregarious, and never treated anyone like a stranger—both of my parents always showed kindness and blessed everyone they could.

When I would ask them, *Why are you so nice to that person or family?* they both told me the same thing: "We are blessed, so fortunate to have a wonderful family. It is important to be grateful and share kindness with everyone we can because not everyone has had a good life. By being kind and looking for the good in others, you may be able to save someone's life."

My dad would say, "Son, it really is D.I.Y. Zen, and life is way too short to be miserable. Always look for the good in people. Be as happy, kind, and Zen for yourself, loved ones, and everyone that you can. Be grateful and share the love and blessings you have received under grace. I love you, Son."

To this day, I love being what I call a *Good Finder* like my dad; he always looked for and pointed out the good he saw and identified in someone, then made a point to tell them what he noticed. I still remember how people would light up with happiness and a big smile as they walked away taller and with a spring in their step as they waved and went on with their life. My dad would say, "Son, what a wonderful person we just met. We brightened their day."

My mom would say years after my dad died, "His love, blessings, kindness, and happiness are always here, and I carry them inside me with so much gratitude for him to this day."

It's no wonder that over the decades many of my friends, colleagues, clients, and people I met only one time have said *thank you* for my blessings, kindness, and happy smile—that I made a positive difference in their life. Even though they were serious, I would laugh with a big smile and say, "It must have been good raisin'. You can thank my mom and dad." It certainly helped me through my careers as an investigator, disaster manager, and public safety official.

Years later, retired from my original careers, I'm still a *Good Finder*, the *DIY Zen Guy*, an author, and a *Blessing Giver*. I am still making and sharing the *Heart Dollar Gratitude and Abundance Blessings* that I learned to make twenty years ago from a nice woman when I moved to Washington, D.C. for a job in 2002. As she was teaching me, she said, "When I make these, I put Grandma's love into each of them. You are a priest and Reiki master, put that with your love, blessings, and good energy into each one you make and share." Since then, I've made over 14,000 of them that are around the world, and many individuals have used my D.I.Y. videos to make and share thousands of them too.

Like my mom and dad, I encourage you to practice your own version of D.I.Y. Zen and be a living example of the art of happiness, kindness, blessing, and gratitude. In your own small way, no matter what turning point moment you may be experiencing, you can always make a positive difference in the world and have a lasting impact on someone's life—even with something as simple as a smile and warm *hello*. Thank you and bless you.

◯

Gary Nobuo Niki is retired from National Disaster Emergency Management and Public Safety. He is the author of *D.I.Y. ZEN and The Art of Gentle Emotional Transformation*. Gary is a Priest, Minister, and Licensed Pastoral Provider in the Washington, D.C. metro area. He works with individuals and groups around the world via phone and internet with multiple energy and healing modalities, vocal vibrational toning, and shares the Heart Dollar Gratitude and Abundance Blessings. He would love to hear from you about your story. Find him at GaryNiki.com

CHAPTER 33

The Dark Side of Light

Irisha Pomerantzeff

I was born in beautiful Biarritz, France, into a Russian family at the end of WWII in July of 1946. I can still feel the delightful giggling mirth playing on my mother's lap as she would drop my head down to her feet, pull me up, then tickle my eyelashes with hers.

Life was difficult in Europe after the war. In 1952, we traversed the equator by ship to Brazil. We had a hilariously fun ceremony and celebration at sea.

Between ages six and nine, people praised me for my ease with languages. Portuguese was my third language. I loved school and learning. I began playing classical piano. Music became my own intimate language, my friend in whom I could confide.

Afterwards, my mother became much stricter and more irritable with me. Everything was wrong with me—I curtsied poorly; my neck was dirty. I was obviously flawed. She punished me with her silence. I began resenting her. She and her art were beautiful, so how could I hate her when I loved her so much? The angrier I got at her, the more I disliked myself—not her, *me*.

On September 6, the day before Brazil's Independence Day, the entire family, my sister's friend, my dog, and my older cousin—nine people—crammed into my dad's small car. Off we went to the beach, singing in chorus as usual. I don't remember much about this day except for our joyful singing.

Somehow, I woke up in an all-white room. An older couple in the room kept whispering, "It's tragic!" I was barely awake, but I knew she was gone. *Why did I get angry with her? I am being punished.*

Oh! I am so glad I played for her on my birthday. She loved the music, "Rain." Unlike other music I played, this was a simple piece that I could almost play with two fingers. It echoed the melancholic drumbeat of rain sounds on the piano. From deep within my own soul, my fingers, one-by-one, extracted love from my own heart and sent that love to land in her heart, then straight out the window into the soil outside. It was raining the night I played it.

After that, on my narrow cot at boarding school, I met up with her each night, and we talked heart to heart. That's how I learned to speak in this way. A year later, she came into my dreams and showed me there's no death.

The following year, I began taking the city bus to and from school. I was almost thirteen. The buses were jam-packed-crowded. I was molested more than once: unable to move, squeezed by tall military men in blue uniforms, my head barely above their waist. For decades, I never whispered a word about this. I felt ashamed and confused.

I didn't know this, but I was looking for love in all the wrong places.

A sign for Energy Healing teaching caught my eye. I signed up for a class simply called *Access*. Gary Douglas channeled and taught it. I was on the right track. Healing was my forte. I began healing me.

A spiritual reader told me mother didn't punish me. Her death was her gift of freedom to me, so I could live my own dream. It was quite a turning point to know that the best gifts are often wrapped in dark packages. All this darkness pointed the way to my inner heart, but I couldn't yet see this.

I was living in an old, large trailer built in 1957 atop a mountain in Hot Springs, near Asheville. I accepted a job to work with two men from a local group home. The transformation in them was outstanding—I was fired!

That's how Dominique and I found each other. He was nineteen, born with severe Cerebral Palsy (CP). He could not speak. His body was so deformed he needed support to sit or hold his head up; his fingers couldn't even hold a flower. His face and eyes were beautiful, but I found myself thinking: *Anyone there?*

Stop! I answered myself as I simultaneously accepted to give it a try.

Several weeks later, on a delightfully glorious morning, I was immersed in the sunlight and silence. I sat next to him, holding his hand as he lay in his recliner. I held an inner dialogue:

I will work with you, Dominique. We must find our language.

Talk to him, like you do with animals.

I went into my heart, feeling, observing. For the first time, instead of sadness, I felt love, compassion. Dominique never looked anyone in their eyes. At this point, his eyes grew larger and larger as he observed the space above my left shoulder and to the left of my neck. The more he looked, the more he came alive. His eyes grew larger and larger, and I realized Dominique could see Spirit. I was in. This was our language.

I heard *Mother* in my heart. *Mother? Me?* I asked.

Yes, Mother!

Was I seeing myself outside of my self-fabricated ugliness? The three of us—Dominique, the light and I—were one. I didn't yet realize that somewhere within I had already had a glimpse of my real self, and I was stepping into being me.

Yes, his body was broken, but he certainly wasn't. I saw clearly and wondered who was really taking care of whom.

Within a month, he moved into my house.

Nine years of insanely excruciating, painstaking, physical, and emotional work and of immeasurably rewarding, beautiful work of compassion, caring, forgiveness, and self-realization ensued. The presence and input of Spirit guidance and support became quasi-visible, a palpable partnership including my energy work. One day at a time, Dominique and I found a common whole body, Spirit, and even spoken language to which he responded with his body, feelings, and emotions. I spoke and sang to him often, interrupting and animating the pregnant silence. Our six cats, three dogs, and the adjacent farm horses all participated in the healing work as did the birds, the pond frogs, the bullfrogs, turtles, and fish. We all joyfully worked together.

During the first seven years, his body kept improving, then it reversed course. Regardless of any difficulty, Dominique's veritable, constant signature remained unconditional joy. His face and eyes transfigured as he participated with the invisible (to us) in episodes of joy. Each time, I held my breath, demanding silence during these sacred moments.

After seven years, he began declining. He also acquired zits veritable furuncles. I did everything I knew to remove them to no avail. His body showed signs of deterioration. I knew what was ahead and was in constant communication with Spirit.

Two years later, one evening in February, he began seizing—half hour or less between each seizure. By 7 p.m. I asked: *What's happening?*

He is departing, Spirit answered.

For the next 17.5 hours, Dominique seized like clockwork—each time a grand mal seizure. In between those, I lay down first in my room, later in his.

I felt I was witnessing an amazing labor-intensive birthing of death. As hard as it was, Spirit was present. At 6 a.m., he stopped seizing. He was calm and ready. I called his mom. Around noon, she arrived with her usual electrifying and vivacious energy—crystals and words she'd collected along her way.

I needed a break. I told Dominique *I've loved you, Dominique* and set out for a walk. No sooner had I started when I heard the voice: *Go home! You can walk any time later.*

As I opened the door, his mother greeted me with a glorifying smile. "Irisha," she said, "Dominique passed three minutes after you left." We embraced and erupted into a glorious dance of thanksgiving. Dominique's body lay on the couch, his skin clean, young, literally transfigured. He looked like an eleven-year-old angel of peace, radiating a visible light.

That was February 2007.

This year, 2022, I entered the *Turning Point Moments* program and decided to peek into the book I'd written immediately after his passing—a 180-page compilation of meditations and conversations with Dominique, Spirit, our work, and each other. I knew I'd given him *who he was*. I saw *who I am*.

Omg! I saw what I did with Dominique, what we did with Spirit, and what Dominique and I did for me.

I saw myself—my spirit and my human reflection. Imagine, I'd compiled this book by a threesome authorship of Spirit, Dominique, and myself. My work with Dominique and Spirit has been my best interpreting job ever, the one that gave me a real and clear image of who I am.

The day I read that book was the day of my deep core turning point: I am the love and compassion shining on every page. We all have those shining moments in our lives, and we must dig to uncover them before we can move forward.

Born in France to two Russian parents, **Irisha Pomerantzeff** spent her childhood in Brazil. Having lived as a resident of many countries, she is fluent in multiple languages. She has a degree in Russian Literature and has also studied at the Paris School of

Interpreters and Translators and at the Boston Museum School of Fine Arts. She is currently writing a book chronicling her journey with Dominique, *More Spirit Than Body.*

CHAPTER 34

Funerals, Jealousy, and Desires

Rainbow

I am a daughter of Grace. That was my mother's name. I love my mom, more so than any words can describe.

When she died in March 2004, I felt shocked. I was thirty-three and a half; she was sixty. No one expected her to die, yet she did. Before her death, my mother and I had enjoyed a deep friendship. We were close, and she felt like a dear sister to me.

Grace was living in California and passed away there. The San Jose Chinese Christian Church held a memorial for her towards the end of March, and I took the eighteen-hour flight from Hong Kong to San Francisco via a layover in Seoul to attend.

What happened that day changed my life forever.

At the memorial service, I got an even bigger shock than receiving the news of her death. So many people I didn't know were there. I personally knew about ten of them, and more than 250 people attended. Once they found out I was Grace's daughter, most of them were eager to speak with me and share personal stories of how deeply they felt Grace's love or how much they enjoyed her laughter. I hadn't known Grace formed a deeply meaningful relationship with so many people, and seeing them all there that day surprised and shocked me.

During the service, I was expected to go to the podium to share a message about Grace's life and about who she was for me as a mother. For this purpose, I had written a brief note ahead of time. The final sentence on that note was a promise from me to Grace. I wrote: *Mom, thank you for your legacy of love. I promise to live your legacy of love and pass it on to all whose lives I touch.*

However, when I went to the podium that day and saw the full size of the audience sitting in one place, I froze and teared up. I hadn't been in front of such a large crowd before, and I didn't expect to speak in front of such a large crowd at my mom's funeral. In that instant, I felt gladness, jealousy, and sadness swirling around inside me. This unexpected mix of feelings rendered me speechless as I stood there, even though the note I prepared was in my hand.

I felt sad I had lost my mom.

I felt glad so many people showed up to pay tribute to Grace. They shared with me words of thanks and personal stories of how my mom had touched each of them as a church member and sister in Christ. For this, I felt a deep gladness and appreciation.

I also felt jealous so many people came. Even though having a funeral is not exactly like having a party, deep down I wanted my funeral to be even bigger than Grace's. I wanted more than 250 people there. As I stood speechless with tears rolling down my cheeks, I felt bad for feeling jealous and tried to stop my mind from racing. It didn't work.

The truth was, in that very moment, I was feeling disappointed by how I had lived my own life. More specifically, I felt I had so much unlived potential inside of me; I also felt I could be making a greater contribution to others. If I were honest, what I was thinking to myself then is: *If I died right now, there would not be more than twenty-five people who would come to my funeral.*

When I realized this, my mind seemed to go out of control. It felt like my mind was trying to push away the feeling of jealousy. Then, it raced ahead to do the following:

- I imagined my own death and funeral.
- I formulated a goal of having much more than 250 people attend my funeral.
- I asked myself: *What would it take to have a bigger audience than all these people sitting in front of me now* (as I was standing at the podium)?

I simultaneously answered the question with another thought: *If I want a big funeral, then obviously I desire to live a life of meaning.* I desired to add value to a lot of people; I desired to positively influence them in such a way that they would feel a deep connection with me and feel called to show up when I die.

I couldn't believe thoughts of how to plan a bigger funeral were bouncing around in my head when I was supposed to be reading a message of tribute to my mother Grace.

Today, with the benefit of hindsight, it is clear to me that, in that moment, I had connected deeply to my own desires for how I wanted to live the rest of my life. Yet, standing at the podium, I finally gathered my thoughts, read the prepared note of tribute, and sat back down again. Thankfully, crying is acceptable behavior at church memorial services, and I cried as the service went on while I sat with all I was feeling and experiencing.

I never expected to feel jealousy at my mom's funeral. Having experienced it, what did I learn? From that experience, I have come to understand that each feeling carries with it *the possibility of giving us a deeper insight and awareness.*

For me, I learned the lesson that jealousy brings. I got to see that jealousy hides our true desires. I realized what's underneath the feeling of jealousy is a simple desire of wanting to shout out loud: *I want what that person has!*

As children, if we can say what we want out loud naturally, then we are simply spontaneously communicating with the people around us. You point your fingers at something that captures your attention. You say out loud: *You see this? This is what I want.* Just like that, you have said what you wanted—simply and directly.

The problem is as we grow up, most of us don't have an opportunity to go around and say out loud: *This is what I want* about each and everything we want. We have learned to be silent even when we truly want something, haven't we?

What is the consequence of being silent and not saying what we want?

When our desire to shout out loud is silenced, the desire doesn't go away; it still lives buried inside us, covered up by the feeling of jealousy. In most cases, if we acknowledge and communicate our desires, then we are able to consciously work towards fulfilling our desires. If we do not acknowledge and communicate our desires, then our desires go underground. They become hidden desires.

The less we acknowledge and communicate our desires, the less aware we are of what we want. Eventually, we stop seeing our own desires, and we are left only with feelings of jealousy whenever we see other people having what we want and experiencing what we want to experience.

Have you ever felt jealous? Do you know what I mean?

The simple truth is: If we can connect with what we want directly and say it out loud, then others will know what we want and support us in getting it.

How do we know when a desire is ready to be unearthed? Whenever we feel jealousy, that's our opportunity to dig a bit deeper to unearth the buried, or previously silenced, desire.

In my case, it was seeing my mom having more than 250 people attending her funeral and me saying: *I want that too.* This led me to see that it was the loving and deeply connected relationships she enjoyed while alive that brought those people to Grace's memorial service. So, what I truly desired was not a big funeral after I die. Instead, *what I truly desired was to experience love and connection while I am alive.*

I also became aware the size of the funeral caught my attention not because I wanted a big funeral but because I desired to make a huge impact with my contribution in the world. It dawned on me that everything I desired had something to do with how I am living my life and had very little to do with what kind of funeral there might or might not be after I die.

This new level of awareness gave me an opportunity to let go of what I experienced at the funeral and to focus on living my life instead. Today, I am grateful that during Grace's funeral feelings of jealousy awakened desires in me. Since that moment, those desires have led me to form a deeper connection with my husband and our children and to cofound a company with my husband and impact the lives of more than 10,000 people.

What desires do you have? Are your desires perhaps hidden by jealousy? When you are feeling jealous, are you willing to dig deeper and connect with your own desires?

○

Born in China and raised in the United States, **Rainbow** is the co-founder of Karisma Learning Institute and known as The Wise Lady by her beloved students. She serves as an optometrist, returning people to their unique vision of how to live paradise on Earth *now*. Today, Rainbow resides in Hong Kong with her beloved husband of thirty years; he is known as Chief Papa Allan. Connect with Rainbow at: https://www.ChiefPapa.com/Rainbow

CHAPTER 35

From Breakdown to Breakthrough: The Resilience of the Human Spirit

Archana Reddy

It was early in January 2013, complete with the anticipation and welcome energy of a wonderful new year, new beginnings, and fresh starts. This is the hope and desire of every new season that wells up in the heart of humans. The power of regeneration, renewal, and hope mixed with my trepidation and uncertainty at the same time, as things had been stressful at work for the previous few months. The constant churn was weighing on my spirit, and I could feel the palpable signs of fatigue and overwhelm building up inside.

It was another typical morning as I moved through the morning routine and went through the iterations to get ready for work. Brush teeth—check. Exercise, meditate, get ready, pray, and eat breakfast, preferably healthy—check. Then, I went off to work and pulled into the parking lot of my corporate office. It was around 8 a.m. All signs pointed to just another typical morning at work, and I hoped that it would be another day without any unexpected hiccups.

The day started quite normally with a greeting to coworkers in the offices next door. Then I went to work in my office, sorting through emails, reviewing inboxes, and making priorities for the day in between team meetings. It was about halfway through the workday in the early afternoon when I felt an intense stabbing pain in my lower abdomen. My eyes looked down and saw what was all around me, and I felt nothing but sheer terror—my heart was racing so fast. There was a huge pool of blood, and my clothes were stained as the blood was flowing at such a fast rate. *What the fuck is happening to me? Is this a hemorrhage or what?*

Am I dying? Tears and tears of horror and grief set in. Even though it was not a literal death, my spirit died that day. I shrieked in horror and thought to myself: *How could this happen? I thought I was doing all the right things.*

I grabbed the full box of tissues nearby and wiped my tears as quickly as I could and then ran to the restroom across the hall and gathered as many paper towels as my struggling, shaking hands could hold. I fought hard to keep myself together as I was shaking inside.

Afterward, I proceeded back to my office where I cleaned the floor as fast I could and then started the next round to the bathroom to gather more supplies. This went on for a good thirty minutes until I was so exhausted and drained, I could barely move. My hands felt like lead, and my body was trembling in pain and in uncertainty of what was to come. My whole being was in shock. I did not know what would come next, but I was trying to move as fast as my fragile state would allow.

I immediately called my gynecologist in a huge state of panic and went for an emergency appointment. In panic, I said to her, "I cannot tolerate this situation that has led me to this point." I explained to her in a panicked voice what had happened, and they did a physical examination. It turned out I had fibroids.

Right then and there, I experienced a huge turning point in my life. I had been tolerating, stomaching, and accepting what was actually unacceptable and intolerable, violating every personal boundary. Overt signs of sexism, lack of support, and other forms of less-than-acceptable situations had led me to this point.

My heart was sinking, feeling the grief and horror, and I knew that all this putting everyone else above what my body was telling me—with signs—had led to this point. The overdoing, overworking, and accepting everything dumped on me, both figuratively and literally, caused me to stop in my tracks. I requested that my doctor immediately put me on leave as I was feeling quite fragile, and my health was not negotiable.

I decided I would take medical leave to allow for my own healing, both inner and outer. I wanted more than a short-term, Band-Aid solution to make the discomfort go away and cover up the symptoms. No, this was deep. The wounds were deep, and only a total and full transformation would do.

So, on my medical leave, I started my journey back to wholeness and healing. First, I gave myself quiet time and space to sit with my situation and do absolutely nothing for the first time in over a decade. I finally gave myself *permission* to rest, be still, and to go into the quiet spaces where I could receive guidance from my higher self on the new aligned actions. I meditated and practiced simply being so I could nourish my body and soul.

I spent a few weeks in this deep inner alchemy and space just being, without needing to perform, produce, and always be perfect. I trusted deeply that the next step would reveal itself. Spirit guided me to seek out a healer to go deeper, and I found a direct mentee of Louise L. Hay. I decided to embark on the 30-Day *You Can Heal Your Life Study Course* with Janice. It was amazing. Janice reminded me the importance of self-love and self-care, prioritizing my needs just as much as others'. Week after week, I experienced more healing, more self-discovery, and more self-love. I was like an unfolding beautiful flower whose petals opened wide under the direction of the sun and the supporting elements.

With each drive to and from those sessions, I saw my disheveled former self who was tired and burned out come back to life. First, I saw small signs, like joy coming back, enjoying the wind in my hair, listening to my favorite songs, and getting motivated to go out into nature again and walk. Then, I witnessed bigger signs, like having all my energy return and allowing myself to feel excited about life again.

I was like a small child who had to teach herself to walk again and then to slowly learn to run until becoming self-sufficient. I called upon the qualities of gentleness and grace at this time. By the third week, I could feel incredible self-love, and I also felt light, free, and empowered. And by the end of the first month, joy inhabited the very spaces that had been overwhelmed by grief, fear, and outrage over what happened to me and the toxic unbalanced system that allowed it.

I was completely transformed and ready to embrace the new. And just like magic, everything fell into place with new opportunities and the guidance to move back to my home state. So, I followed the guidance and recreated life anew again.

In the process of breaking down, I had the opportunity to break into wholeness and heal the little girl within—for her to be seen and witnessed and held and healed. She had been crying out for love and validation, to be witnessed and heard. In this safe space, she received all those things.

Janice, who led the program, was an incredible coach and healer. She taught me how to love myself and heal my inner child, so I could make better decisions and learn to trust myself more. This was a powerful journey of transforming pain into healing and wholeness.

The process of being broken down allowed me to become introspective about where I was giving too much, not respecting my own boundaries, and not asserting my own needs to be healthy. Healing takes time, but the human spirit is stronger than any circumstance, so I learned. More importantly, I learned the value of self-love and self-respect, as well as learning to navigate the fine line between self-care and responsibility so that all aspects of the self could be in balance.

The process of breakdown to breakthrough can be painful and vulnerable, but if you are willing to shine a light into those dark spaces, there is much to be learned and much healing is available. On the other side is a transformation of yourself into a more empowered version who can set better boundaries. Remember, it is okay to not be okay with something. A decision is just that; it can be changed if it means your health and well-being are being impacted. This is another key lesson—learning when to stay and when to pivot to honor yourself.

Lastly, over the years since this experience, I have learned that this process of taking your power back is iterative, and life will give you many opportunities to see if you have really learned the lesson by putting new characters and situations your way. The pain is temporary, but the lessons can be permanent. It is an individual journey of unfolding, and every experience will create more of who you are and meant to be. In retrospect, the process continued for another decade, but it also unlocked my most potent gifts of healing, coaching, and becoming more of my authentic self.

The journey towards healing and wholeness starts from within and ripples outwards. Every challenge is an opportunity to heal something within that is mirrored in our environments. We can choose to heal or stay stuck in anger, grief, and all the negative emotions. The human spirit is capable of transforming again and again and again until the lessons are finally learned, never to be repeated.

Archana Reddy is a creative and spiritual soul who has been on the spiritual path for over a decade and seeks to work with creatives, visionaries, and out-of-the-biz thinkers who seek to tap into their soul purpose and master their inner and outer reality. In the last three years, she has been certified in Executive Coaching, Laser Coaching, and trained in various healing modalities including pranic/theta healing (basic DNA/advanced DNA), advanced medical intuition, matrix regeneration technique, and dreamporting level 1 and is currently studying Quantum Healing, Dreamporting Mastery, and GeoHealing energy work.

CHAPTER 36

How a Broken Heart Led Me Back to Wholeness

Miriam Reilly

His piercing chocolate-brown eyes were the first thing I noticed. It was a Friday evening, and we were at a crowded bar in Dublin city center, close to the bank where we both worked. A mutual colleague introduced us. I felt an instant attraction. We began dating that night, and a few years later, we got married and started our family.

Then on a cold, grey Wednesday morning in November 2008, everything changed.

I returned home after the school drop-off to collect a few things before going into the city for work. All was quiet: the morning rush of cornflakes, lunches, scrambling to find shoes, and tie shoelaces was over. Running up the stairs, I turned the corner and froze.

My husband's body lay lifeless on the stairs leading up to the attic. His familiar brown eyes appeared to be looking straight at me, but the light was gone out of them. I rushed forward, reaching for his left wrist. Unable to find a pulse, I fell to the ground sobbing. Soon after, the emergency services arrived and confirmed that his heart had stopped beating.

My mind was racing fast: how would I explain what had happened to our boys? They adored him. He was their hero.

He'd left us in the weak light of a November morning without saying goodbye or leaving a note. It seemed so abrupt and unbearably cruel. His death catapulted me into an unfamiliar and frightening place. I had no reference points or map to help me find my way out. Months passed in a blur. I was existing in a desolate no-man's-land of grief and confusion. This was not the life I had expected to be living in my mid-thirties.

All I knew was that one part of my life was over. And the next hadn't yet begun.

In the quiet of night as I lay awake, I became aware of a small quiet voice inside me. It urged me to keep moving forward, not to give in to the despair I sometimes felt engulfing me. The voice promised me that one day I would be in a better place. I would become stronger and wiser and be able to use my experience to help others.

I decided to trust it. I started to believe that I could heal—and be happy again. That belief would prove to be the catalyst for my healing journey.

I started therapy. Deep inner work demands courage and persistence. I would make good progress only to suffer a debilitating setback. At times, I felt completely stuck. I'd peel back one layer of damaging beliefs only to find several more lurking beneath, but I knew I had crossed a line.

There would be no going back.

Therapy fostered greater self-awareness in me. I began to feel more optimistic about my future. Something inside me had shifted, but there was still some way to go.

Reared in Catholic Ireland in the 1970s and 1980s, religion had played a central role in my early life. However, by my twenties, I had started to drift from the Catholic Church as shocking revelations began to surface. I was so preoccupied with my busy career and small children that I hadn't noticed how spiritually impoverished I had become. When I left the corporate world to focus on getting my life back on track, I had more time to check in with myself.

The yearning to find a deeper meaning to life became impossible to ignore.

There is something in the depths of our being that hungers for wholeness.
— Thomas Merton

I began my journey in search of meaning with a two-year training in spiritual development. We met for residential weekends in a soul-nourishing setting in the shadows of the Wicklow Mountains. The training compelled me to do some deep self-examination. We studied the development of the chakra system in depth from birth onwards. I started to understand how early childhood events shape emotional development. I came to appreciate how early trauma informs symptoms—mental and physical—later in life.

I felt drawn to learning about ancient Vedic philosophy. I signed up for a month-long meditation retreat in the Himalayas in Pokhara, Nepal. Far from the comforts of my Western life, we rose before dawn to sit still (on a cold concrete floor) for long periods. I studied ancient yoga philosophy and pranayama. I endured the horrors (no exaggeration) of sugar withdrawal as my body adjusted to a simple and repetitive diet of rice and vegetables. I discovered how much easier life flowed when I released attachments and adopted an attitude of acceptance.

I returned home after that month lighter in both body and spirit. It was another watershed moment. Having experienced another way of being in the world—one characterized by simplicity, presence, and self-discipline, there was no going back to my old ways.

I deepened my spiritual practice with training courses in the US, becoming a certified yoga nidra teacher in Massachusetts and a certified transpersonal and spiritual hypnotherapist in North Carolina. I spent several weeks in a remote jungle in Panama (with one of my sons) and developed resilience and self-reliance. Far from the distractions of the modern world, I continued on my journey home to my true self.

I also trained in London as a transformational hypnotherapist, delving deep into the power of the subconscious mind to heal and transform us. I came to understand that the meaning we attach to what has happened to us is more important than the actual events themselves. By changing the meaning, by rewriting our personal narrative, we can set ourselves free. This was a huge insight for me. Rather than being stuck in our old narrative, we have the freedom to create a new one and to break free of the victim mentality.

The next step on my spiritual journey opened me up to the power of music to bring harmony and balance to our body, mind, and soul. While I was solo traveling in the Middle East, I was first introduced to Tibetan healing bowls. I discovered I was able to enter a state of profound relaxation during a sound bath unlike anything I'd experienced before. I could access higher realms of consciousness with ease.

I knew this was something I had to explore further, so when I returned home to Ireland, I began attending sound baths at every opportunity. In time, I studied at the British Academy of Sound Therapy (BAST). As well as restoring balance, sound healing helps us enter a deep meditative state. I am certain that the future of healing is sound.

Connecting more and more with my spiritual side has proven to be a journey with no end. I've had the privilege of working with some gifted teachers along the way. My life falling apart on that November day years ago put me on a path of self-exploration and coming home to myself. The life I have now is so different from the life I'd imagined for myself: it's fuller, more expansive, and imbued with meaning.

Often, it's a traumatic event that stops us in our tracks and breaks us open. A divorce, a job loss, or the death of a loved one can act as a doorway into our inner world. Pain and suffering can be the catalyst for deep change, but the truth is that *every moment has within it the potential to create a turning point in our lives.*

We can awaken to our spiritual selves by establishing a simple daily meditation practice. Having a spiritual practice adds depth and meaning to our often rushed lives. When we put down our phones and take the time to sit with our busy minds and fidgety bodies, we transform our ordinary lives into something sacred.

Establishing a deep connection with yourself changes everything. You can do this work anywhere; you don't need to travel to the snow-capped Himalayas or to the humid jungles of Central America like I did. All you need is a desire to come home to yourself and to get to know the real you—for the very first time. Becoming whole is the purpose of your journey. The path is different for each of us, but the endpoint is always the same. Taking the first step, by committing to ten minutes a day of quiet time to meditate or attending a weekly yoga class, can be the way home to yourself. A life of joy, presence, and connectedness awaits you. You'll never look back.

Miriam Reilly is a writer, immersive meditation teacher, and transpersonal hypnotherapist living in West Cork, Ireland. She guides people to a place of deep healing using spiritual regression to explore events and experiences in early childhood, womb time, and past lives. She also shares her work through online courses, eBooks, meditation audios, and hypnotic audios. Her mediation audio, "Healing Sanctuary" is available to download for free at miriamreilly.mykajabi.com

CHAPTER 37

From Primal Scream to Living the Dream

Patrick Smyth

Recently, I promised forty some people that I would co-write a book to be published in June. I have never been an author, so I was scared. *What the hell am I doing?* I kept asking myself. Yet, I did it anyway, and suddenly my fear became so intense that I felt sick to my stomach. All of my internal conversations crushed together and became inaudible. I was engaged in a primal scream—a scream for my very existence.

As soon as our team call was over, I ran to the golf course where I've been hiding out for years, working on getting better. Needless to say, I played a lousy game of golf. I played like a tortured soul, who only seeks more misery. *Why did I make this promise?*

My friend Britt, who recently won The NYC Big Book Award for the best sociology book of 2021, *The Master Book of MEMES*, has been telling me for years, "You're running from something."

I shooed his ideas away as BS. Yet, here I was, trying to figure out, *How do I get out of this one? I did contact these folks in order to support me in writing a book. So, why am I so scared?*

When I left the golf course, I was still feeling this impending doom, so I began to think of things that could remove this excruciating feeling. I could get drunk, watch TV, or go to a movie. *Omg! I sound like a kid trying to get out of doing his homework.*

Finally, I capitulated and admitted to myself that I was trying to hide, fleeing something, but I wasn't in the clear yet. Panicking, I switched gears and began to think of other types of excuses. I told myself that I only knew one of the other authors in the book, so it wouldn't matter if I quit.

And then, I heard a different voice say, *And nobody matters to you, anyway, do they?* I looked at my life and found proof galore. I have no significant other, my daughter no longer talks to me, and I can't see my grandson. Many of my old friends like me, but we don't talk about much—we golf. Most of my siblings have separated themselves, few of my former employees speak kindly of me—none ever became friends —and now I live somewhere where I know nobody. So, this is my life? *What gives?*

So, I called my friend Alex. I explained my dread and the circumstances I thought brought it on. "I really want to fix this," I said. "I want to be free of this feeling and these circumstances."

Alex asked, "What are you afraid of?"

"I don't know," I confessed.

He responded, "Well, where will all the problems you're worried about occur—in your past, present, or future?"

I answered, "In the future, sometime later?"

"Exactly! They haven't even happened yet, and you are afraid of them. You're afraid of what *might* occur. Do you know if you'll even live long enough to write a story? Did you wake up two days ago and say, *I'm going to feel petrified of giving my word to write a story?* You are living like your past predicts your future. Can you see that you put all your fears into the future? Since things didn't work out before, you're afraid to give them another go. You are petrifying your own life!"

I replied, "Yes, that's true."

He asked about my last writing assignment. I told him I had sent a chapter of the book I wanted to write to three people, including him. Everyone had responded by telling me they liked my style and encouraging me to continue.

He said, "Now we are getting somewhere. It isn't the promise you made, and it's not the consequences in the future because you can't predict them. So, now, in the space of not knowing, look at your past life as an examination."

Though I didn't know how it happened, the fear was gone, and I had a whole new opening and context in which to start reviewing my life. As I looked back, I saw a suffering child, a tortured teenager, a lost young adult, and, finally, someone who tried and tried and tried and couldn't get out of his own way. I saw nothing of my accomplishments—even though I ran a successful company, am retired, and can take care of myself. I ran several marathons, some of which were in the former Soviet Union. I have a beautiful and successful daughter, a handsome and loving grandson, and I play golf rather well. I have a successful life. So, I asked myself, *Why am I so afraid of what others will think about me?*

I continued looking at my past, remembering that Alex told me to be clinical with it. I had never examined my past this way; I simply had memories and saw them as the truth. Now, I searched for how I was acting, thinking, and feeling. *What were my emotions, moods, and so on?* I was no longer the victim of my circumstances; I was an examiner.

I remembered being a happy, go-lucky child up until the age of four. One night, I couldn't sleep, and, looking up through the top window next to the cathedral-shaped ceiling, I saw a white dove with a halo around its entire body. Since I was being marinated in religious energy, I immediately knew I was being visited by the Holy Ghost

(Spirit). In awe, I told myself, *I am someone special*. I held onto that moment and told myself that I was meant for an important purpose.

Fast forward about three years. My older brother and I were walking in the woods when we ran into three of the older boys in the wider neighborhood. They asked us to join them. My brother said no and headed home. I stayed.

After a little talking, the one I knew the best pulled out his penis. He told me I had to suck on it, or he'd have this mean old man in the neighborhood kill me. The mere mention of this old man scared the daylights out of all of us little kids. I believed in order to save myself, I had to do this awful thing for this kid, or I was going to be killed. I did it and ran home as fast as possible on those little legs of mine.

In that moment, I lost all of my *specialness*, and, for me, it meant I had lost everything. I was then enveloped in a cloud of shame, guilt, and embarrassment. I was no longer shielded by being a special child of God. I was sure my parents and God knew, and I would be punished.

As an adult, I realized with amazement I had been traumatized. I recalled and relived the shame I felt about myself. I saw and experienced the feelings as the child I had been. That child and the adult I had grown up to be really were—and still are—petrified with fear. It dawned on me that I have been waiting all this time for that punishment to happen. No wonder I've been so paralyzed in my life.

I physically hugged myself and told myself, *Everything is all right now. I don't have to be afraid anymore.* No one was going to kill me. *Everything is going to be okay.*

Then, I remembered I made up that my parents withdrew from me. Now, I realized that I withdrew from everyone, including myself. I stopped dreaming and planning for my future. And even though the mean old man is long gone and my parents are dead, I was still expecting to be killed or punished. Wow!

So, with my homework done, I called Alex. The first thing out of Alex' mouth was, "So, you dug a well of shame, and you've been trying to live a life from the bottom of that well? Unless you had seen it for yourself and relived the experience, you would not have gotten anything out of my telling you."

I said, "I feel really good and ready to go! But will I feel any more shame or fear?"

"The well is much shallower now, and you have the ladder to climb out and stop being miserable. Now, you can handle it."

I thanked him profusely, and he thanked me for doing the work. With my promise kept, all things are, once again, special in the world.

Socrates said, "An unexamined life is not worth living." Now, I invite you to the journey from primal scream to living the dream. Joyfully, I recommend tackling all of life by questioning everything that seems locked in truth, without blaming anyone or anything for what seems to be taunting you. As for me, I intend to stay in the question long after I think I know the answers.

A native of Maryland, **Patrick Smyth** is a graduate of Erhard Seminars Training (*est*) and the Landmark Forum for breakthrough being. Patrick ran a construction company for twenty-five years and ran marathons as well. He currently supports the Last Judgement Day sans Armageddon, wishing peace for all and everyone. He golfs to explore peacefulness and supports the planting of native flora.

CHAPTER 38

Do You Want Breakfast, Son?

Irina Sotirova

E ven now when I remember her story, I still hear her sweetly inviting voice, "Iriiii, do you want to have breakfast, son?"

Maria used to call me *son* every now and then, and I never quite understood why, but I loved it. I loved every single expression of it, and I grinned every time I heard it. My sister and I joked, giggled, and winked at each other because gender apparently meant nothing to Maria. I now believe that *son* was an expression of love for her—a word that unified it all, a reference of affection regardless of the gender—that she liked to use, and I never found the need to object.

She was generous and loving and cheerful and chatty, and I liked looking into her eyes that were the colour of honey spilt over a fertile earth, gently wrinkled around the corners by the kindness of her nature, as I waited impatiently to hear a story that she so readily told every time she was babysitting. I loved most the one of her own life. I curiously flipped the pages of the old album with black-and-white photos that she liked to show, looking at her image from the years back—young and confident, wearing a long dress, flowers in her hair, and a smile that said: *I've got you, world!*

Beautiful in her younger years, popular and sought after for her looks, her wit, and her gentle and compassionate spirit, she had all the suiters that a girl in a small village could possibly ask for. "Everyone liked my golden curls," Maria used to tell us, confident even at an old age, and it was not difficult for me to believe it. While flipping the yellowing pages of that album, I discovered the light of that face still emanating from the faded old photos. "And everyone asked me to dance at all the socials, everywhere I went," she added proudly.

I remember her constantly buying the wicker baskets that local women offered in a loud voice at the front gate. Despite the kindness of her soul, she had been a willful and often stubborn young woman, living as if no ache could keep her away from smiling and dancing, as if no physical disadvantage could hinder her dynamic soul. So, when a pain was ignored for a while and home remedies did not give the expected relief, she was brought to the hospital with a most severe case of peritonitis. The doctors fought to overcome the infection, barely saving her life. In the quiet tiptoeing of the others around her, she sensed a cruel verdict waiting to be heard—the verdict that she would never have children.

When her beloved one, studying abroad, received the letter with her heartfelt confession, he sent back his farewell words, leaving her inconsolable. Her older sister then promised their dying mother that Maria would be looked after as no man would ever marry a woman that misfortunate.

The word spread around the village with the speed of light; no secret could be kept, no one could be spared, no matter how adored and sought after by the most eligible bachelors a woman was. Her life was unmistakably turned upside down.

"I was devastated for the love I lost and for the children I would never have," her big soft eyes filled with tears and her wrinkles grew deeper as Maria spoke.

It was a colourful and mystic dusk when Dimitar came, a foreign villager, riding on his motor bike. He came to the gatherings every weekend to quietly admire her gracefulness. He knew nothing of the story, at least not at first. He fell in love with the hints of honey dipped in her eyes and the curls bouncing around the gentle features of that saddened face—ever so appealing and bright.

He was kind but strong-willed; his voice was deep but never loud. His words were rarely spoken, but people were eager to hear them and so was she. Like two forces of nature, they were: she the wildfire of life—dancing, burning, expanding, willful, and compelling—and he the deep grounding soil—reliable, inviting, committing, wrapping, nurturing, and always ready to catch every fall.

Soon, the *Will you marry me?* came. When she whispered back, "You will never have children if you marry me," tears crawled down her honey-earth eyes.

"I know, love, I know. You are what I want. You are enough—you always will be enough." He sheltered her in his arms.

They created a warm, inviting, and sacred space for each other where acceptance, love, and joy melted into a homey serenity that came with the deep belief that they were complete.

I now trust that it was that moment of *yes* that turned acceptance into abundance, friendship into love, and love into light. The choices of Maria and Dimitar opened up a portal for a miracle seeking to emerge.

"Do you want some breakfast, son?" she sang out from the kitchen while I was reading a book and dangling my feet on the tiny, engraved chair that Grandpa got for me from the gypsy market. How I loved that chair! And how I loved that soniferous voice coming from the kitchen accompanied by the smell of *mekitsi*, the best breakfast I have ever had.

Even now, so many years after Maria has gone, I can still smell and taste the fried warm dough with the melting cheese inside. Oh, how have we tried to recreate that simple-as-it-may-seem recipe, but we never quite managed to.

Do you want breakfast, son? I still hear the ringing tones, sounding a bit concerned when I did not reply. I can see Maria popping her head in the crack of the squeaky old door, looking quizzically at me dangling my feet on the little engraved chair.

A son she had and a daughter, and a son of a son, and daughters of a daughter. Every now and then, she lovingly called all of them *son*, gender completely ignored. Whether it was the desire for a child, the gift of the accepting love, or the magical blend of kindness and support that was channeled through that word, I would never know, but I was wrapped in light every time I heard it.

I was not wondering about all that back when Maria was preparing breakfast. I was simply sitting on that little engraved chair from the gypsy market—that little chair that Dimitar bought for me—but I always replied, "I'm coming right now, Grandma!" grinning every time.

That grin on my face, every tiny spot, every single cell that shaped the wholeness of my being are the minuscule miracles gifted from Maria's loving soul. I sit quietly on a much larger chair now, but still wrapped in the memories of her existence and in the notion that when the light is dimmed and the worlds are collapsing, despair becomes the organic response. Then our own acceptance—of the way nature lovingly molds us with all creation hidden in the pain of challenging turns—brings us closer to the answers we seek and grants us gifts beyond perception.

That flow of self-acceptance gives sense where logic seems lost, creation where healing is scarred with the *impossible* mark, and brightness where darkness appears infinite. Then love picks you up and leads you to places miraculous and startling, places where you find yourself and your essence intwined with another being, the potion that bears togetherness for the generations to come. Lean in and listen as life seeks to spark hope and to signal the next step forward, and trust—trust that magic is there for you, too, as it was for Maria and Dimitar, and me. Invite it, seek it, find it, and let yourself be written by the hand of the loving Universe.

Every so often when I look in the mirror, I smile that I never got Maria's golden curls, as she quite vocally hoped for while swirling my hair around her fingers, and I remind myself of her story. Then the moment came for me to walk down a park alley pondering a decision and a choice that was pressing to be made when I stumbled upon it, on a wall of a tiny building, carefully tucked between the trees. *Cree en la magia y la encontrarás* (Believe in magic and you will find it), I read on the wall, and even though she never spoke a word of Spanish, I never doubted the gentle touch of her loving soul, the warmth of her never-fading light from above, and the answer I already knew.

Irina Sotirova is a traveler, adventurer, and believer of the sacredness of the soul search. This story is the inspiration and the gateway to her forthcoming children's book *Light for Iris* (LightForIris.com), a bouquet of mindfulness short stories. In a girly pure and magical way, she welcomes others into a world of warmth and connectedness seasoned with a pinch of homey coziness and a promise for peace and love.

CHAPTER 39

Widow's Bridge

Kat Wells

"Time of death, 11:31 p.m.," the doctor said. My husband of twenty-eight years was gone. Forever. And so was my life. It felt like a trap door had opened beneath me, and I was falling with no place to land.

Over the past three years, I had mourned the loss of my mother, my young brother-in-law, and three close friends. I thought I knew grief, knew what to expect, but my depth of pain was so great, I didn't know if I would survive it this time.

A nurse guided me out of the room to her desk. "I know it's late, and this is difficult for you, but time is of the essence. Would you be willing to donate Mark's organs?" she asked.

For a moment, I snapped back to reality. "Of course, absolutely. What do I need to do?"

As she guided me through the process of filling out a health questionnaire and release forms, I found myself thinking: *What am I doing? What if Mark's still alive? What if this is all a mistake?*

Even though I had held his hand as they removed the respirator and he took his last breath, even though I felt the life leave his body, my mind would not accept that he was gone.

I moved through the next few days in a trance. I'd wake up in the mornings, expecting to see Mark next to me, forgetting for a few seconds what had happened, and then cruel reality returned. I felt as if I was in a perpetual fog, walking in mud up to my knees. My thoughts and words seemed to be in slow motion. I could feel nothing. I was like a paper doll, flat and lifeless.

My state of mind frightened me. I had always been the strong one, the organizer, the planner, the guide, the rock for others. I could always find hope in situations even when others gave up. Until now.

Hope is being able to see that there is light despite all the darkness.
— Desmund Tutu

When Mark was diagnosed with *pulmonary fibrosis*, I hoped that he would beat the odds even though the doctors said there was no cure and he had just a short time to live. We were living in a miracle as months turned into years, and he seemed to be doing well.

But, three years after his diagnosis, he suffered a ruptured appendix and, after surgery, developed sepsis that triggered the development of fibroids in his lungs. Once the sepsis was under control, the doctor said there was nothing more they could do and sent us home.

I refused to give up hope, and while we were waiting for the hospital to finish their discharge procedures, I researched local pulmonary specialists. It was a miracle that I found one that had received a cancellation and could take us immediately. So, I loaded Mark into his wheelchair, grabbed his oxygen tank, wheeled him to my Jeep, and we drove two blocks to the university hospital.

We spent several hours filling out paperwork, speaking with the doctor, and running tests. Once the test results came back, the doctor explained that Mark's lungs were rapidly filling with fibroids and that because of his low lung capacity, he was now eligible to apply for a lung transplant. It was his only hope to survive.

Before he could be accepted into the program, he would have to go through days of testing to determine if he was physically and mentally a good candidate for the transplant. Normally, it would take months, but the doctor knew Mark didn't have much time, so they checked him into a private room on the pulmonary floor of the hospital to expedite the process.

Throughout the testing, I held onto hope. Finally, we received the miraculous news that he qualified and had been moved to the top of the donor list because of his urgent need. Now, all we could do was wait and hope that a matching donor would be found in time.

At the hospital, I spent hours in meetings with Mark's team of doctors and kept detailed records for them since Mark could no longer remember what the doctors told him. He was in pain. His life was slowly draining away, and there was nothing I could except keep hoping for a miracle.

Then, one day in February, the miracle happened. We got the call that a donor match had been found. Everyone rushed into action. We were given permission and consent forms to sign, and the surgeons and support staff were called in to prep for the surgery.

The staff let us know the lungs had arrived and they would be taking Mark into surgery soon. As I prepared to leave the pre-op holding area, the surgeon walked into the room. We knew something was wrong by the look on his face.

"I'm so sorry to tell you this, but the lungs were compromised. We won't be able to do the surgery," he said. Tears welled up in the doctor's eyes as he turned and walked away. Mark's body shrunk into his hospital bed. After four longs months of preparing and waiting, we both knew his time had run out. All hope vanished.

We pretended to be optimistic for each other because we couldn't bear to speak the truth. Within hours, the pain drugs were no longer working, and he suffered an embolism. They had to intubate him and put him in a coma to relieve his suffering. I knew he was leaving me. I wanted to climb into bed next to him, but I couldn't. The slightest movement of the bed set off all the warning buzzers on the life support machines. All I could do was sit by his side and hold his hand.

I waited for Mark's friends and family to make it to the hospital to say their good-byes before I gave the hospital permission to turn off the machines. It was the worst thing I have ever had to do in my entire life. As he took his last breath, I felt something in me die.

In the moment I became a widow, my previous life faded away. After Mark's passing, most of the relationships we had as a couple seemed to vanish overnight. Friends we had traveled the world with, celebrated with, and spent over a decade of our lives with disappeared.

At first, I was confused and hurt. How could everyone abandon me during the worst time of my life? And then I realized, those who loved me were lost too. They didn't know what to do or say. We were no longer on common ground.

For over two years, I felt I was on a bridge between two worlds, the widow's bridge. On one end was my old life, the one I could never go back to. On the other end was the new life that I couldn't yet imagine. The fog of grief covered my path and clouded my vision. I took my time and traveled slowly to keep my footing as best I could.

I didn't know how long it would take to cross the bridge to my new life. Some days I could almost see the other side, but then I'd turn around and head back towards the past, toward the familiar, hoping I could return to my old life. But there was nothing there. It had all disappeared. All that was left was the bridge.

The widow's bridge was also a bridge of miracles. I didn't notice them at first, until I began to have visitors on the bridge. Most were kind strangers who helped me on my journey. Mark's respiratory specialist, Fernando, showed up at my front door to ask how he could help. For two months, he sorted, organized, and cleared out two garages and a private storage room full of Mark's classic cars, tools, trailers, machinery, and thirty years of projects.

Chris, a potential buyer for one of Mark's cars, who happened to be a home builder, came to my rescue to repair and remodel my bathroom after it was damaged by a massive water leak and no one else would take the job.

My financial advisor, accountant, real estate agent, and attorney took care of my finances, probating the will, selling my old home, and finding me a new one.

A nurse from the hospital mailed me a letter letting me know that two people gained their eyesight because of Mark's organ donation.

A coffee barista drew funny faces in the cream of my coffee to make me laugh.

There were mourning miracles every day, and with each miracle, I took one more step across the widow's bridge. Even Mark showed up on the bridge. I was having trouble locating the title to one of his classic cars. It wasn't with the other car titles and was probably misfiled in one of six large filing cabinets.

The thought of searching through all those files was overwhelming. So, I asked out loud, "Mark, where the heck did you put the title?" And a picture of a metal cabinet with a wood top came to mind. As I flipped through the files, I passed one labeled *auto insurance*, and heard, "Go back." Smiling, I went back and reached into the file and found the title envelope tucked in the bottom.

The widow's bridge was a necessary part of my journey back to wholeness, a shedding of my old identity. It showed me that I was supported in my life, and I began to trust again, hope again, laugh and smile again.

Today is the four-year anniversary of Mark's passing, and my life is more beautiful than I could have ever imagined. The void left by loss was fertile ground to bring in something fresh and new. I have experienced more happiness, success, connection, excitement, and love than ever before.

A new man has entered my life who understands my loss. We will be married in a few months, and the bond of love we share is held on common ground. It's no coincidence that his wife passed away a few days before Valentine's Day and Mark passed two days after, just one week apart.

No matter where you are in life or how devastating your grief has been, don't listen to the fear. Focus on the little mourning miracles each day brings, and trust the bridge is leading you to a life more beautiful than the one you left behind.

Best-Selling Author, Certified Hypnotherapist, and Master Life Coach, **Kat Wells** graduated summa cum laude from Texas A & M University and trained under Dr. Sue Morter, founder of Morter Institute for BioEnergetics. Kat is a certified Energy Codes Master Trainer and founder of Kat Wells International. She provides coaching, seminars, and workshops worldwide, using her knowledge and skills to empower individuals and organizations to realize their full potential. If you're ready to love your life, visit Kat at her website: KatWellsInternational.com

CHAPTER 40

Collapsing into Miracles

Jamie Leno Zimron

I grew up in a waterhole,
though always wished I could have lived
on the lip of a perpetually breaking wave.

So said my restless, brooding teenage psyche in an English essay at the factory-like high school I couldn't wait to leave to get on with living. Desperately longing for aliveness, I set out determined for non-stop highs on that exhilarating lip.

It's cool fantasy and nice poetry, but surfers know they mostly paddle and wait to catch a workable wave for as long as the breaker lasts. Then it's more paddling and waiting for a next thrilling but brief ride atop a wave that always crests, dissolves, and disappears.

Peak moments are part of many more daily grind and rest times. There is a rhythm to things I had yet to comprehend. Going 24/7 was not enough; I went all out 25/8 and wished for a world of 36/10. I studied and taught voraciously, ran my own martial arts school, had a somatic psychotherapy practice, was a golf champion and

239

social change activist, helped introduce Aikido into Russia, worked with institutes and universities, jogged daily, ran rivers, guided rafts, backpack traveled, climbed a few mountains, took up the banjo, spoke three languages, and deeply loved my family and friends.

Like most driven people, I was busy, breathless, and could hardly keep up with myself. From my dad, I learned to work and play hard as a badge of honor. To stop or chillax was unthinkable. I even practiced Aikido—The Art of Peace—like a fanatic.

It was all so good—except for devastating migraines, accumulating injuries, and escalating inner angst. Something was definitely the matter. Itching to spread my wings wider still, I took apart my together life in San Francisco and moved to Israel. This was the Oslo Accords era, so I eagerly imported my work and dove into activity. But we really do take ourselves with us wherever we go, and my overdone energy continued undoing me. I was burning my adrenals and all my growth and peace efforts to a crisp. Trying to be better, do more, and live to the hilt, I was getting worse and killing myself.

Breakdown finally hit, stopping me since I couldn't stop myself. I was so off-kilter and exhausted that I crashed and burned out, badly. Far from ever-cresting waves, I washed ashore, sick and sore, in a heap of what a naturopathic doctor termed adrenal collapse. Allopaths and just folks call it a nervous breakdown. It woke me up. The diagnosis was true, and I was completely debilitated.

Nervous system wipeout is hell. Along with my adrenals, my busy life and ego collapsed. I was totally sidelined, my identity and credentials in smithereens. Sleep and work were impossible. I could hardly eat or act at all. Under the overload of stress biochemicals, it was unbearable to be around anyone, go anywhere, or simply be in my body. Trudging to a friend's Thanksgiving feast, I had to excuse myself to go curl up and hide in her bed. An intrepid traveler, the mere thought of being on an airplane or trip made me shudder. I was an overwhelmed, clinical wreck, totally lost to my usual extroverted, high-achieving, happy self.

Rattling around in limbic stress-brain, all seemed gloomy and gone. I was in the valley of the shadow without a hint of a brighter horizon or way back to health. Chasing the unrealistic dream of nonstop ecstatic surfing through life soured into utter nightmare. Attachment to it had superseded all my training and better knowing.

And yet, something far bigger and smarter was going on, much beyond what my mind and ego knew about life and how to live it. Whether seen or believed or not, this seems true for us all. We hear we are *not* our bodies or minds, but a non-material yet palpable universal spirit-energy animating us and everything. Some call it Ki, Chi, or Kundalini, an energy coming from an invisible, yet ever-present creative power named God, Source, The All, The One. Without allegiance to any system or words, there is consensus around a vast, intelligent energy of life itself that we do our best to glimpse through religions, secular and scientific studies, and spiritual mysteries.

My experience is that we are living in and attuned to a vibrantly smart energy-cosmos all around and within us. Even during my body and soul's darkest nights, its nature felt divine. I could sense being on an inevitable and guided journey into happier, healthier wholeness. The process was uneven and took some years. Often it felt awful, like crossing a terrible depressing desert to a doubtful promised land. Yet magic kept happening, making every step of my seemingly impossible way possible. Some unseen genius provided detailed miracles of synchronistic support to bring me through the long dark valley. Ever since, it has me laughing incredulously: *What are the chances?!*

One day in a kitchen in Jerusalem, a friend mentioned San Diego. I saw an unprecedented flash of light that sparked a massive turning point. Though not a SoCal kind of gal, I decided to take a six-month healing sabbatical that turned into sixteen amazing, transformational San Diego years—although it all got off to a scary start.

Alone and unmoored, I tried making new friends by joining a wellness program. Instead, a too-deep colon cleanse threw me into metabolic mayhem and off the adrenal cliff. I felt insanely anxious and in need of a physical or maybe mental hospital. Thank goodness I had been referred to a naturopath for post-cleanse diet advice. It felt like my car drove me to her for help. Sure enough, she accurately spotted my adrenal disaster. Sparing me a hospital, she let me hang out in her office for a month while treating my nervous system to calm and even out.

Aching and totally sidelined from shoulder, back, and hip injuries, I was led to the creator of BLISS Fitness: Balance Lengthen Integrate Stretch Strengthen. The teacher was excellent and the exercises so powerful that my physical pains steadily subsided and function began returning. Meanwhile, someone asked if I wanted to meet a Jewish lesbian. *Ya think?!* She managed massage therapy at an upscale hotel, hired me, and we became girlfriends for several meant-to-be years. Incredibly, healing was happening, and I had work, income, and love to help me recover.

We meditated together, discovered the healing powers of essential oils, exchanged bodywork, ate well, hiked, drummed, and rented a round house that felt like living in a warm womb. Not only that! As the new LGBTQ theater Artistic Director, she was approached by a gay Palestinian man to stage his play *Salaam Shalom*, that tackled Arab-Jewish territorial and cultural conflicts. For me, bereft leaving the Middle East, the play miraculously manifested as the most meaningful project imaginable.

In my darkest hours, I berated myself as a failure to my family, but my brother, sister, and mother made special visits to San Diego. My hard-working father shocked me with his support: "You know, great people go through breakdowns, then do their greatest work later in life. So don't worry; your best days are coming!"

And then—my girlfriend and I broke up. Anxiety, agony, and despair flooded back in. Without a clue where or what next, I sat crying one dreary day on a lonely lagoon bench. Suddenly, I felt a giant unbidden balloon burst and break free in my head as something said: *It could take forever to therapize and fix every issue you have, so just let go and move on.* That afternoon, I bumped into an acquaintance who was looking for a roommate. By evening, I had a new home in her ocean-cove condo and felt ready for my next big life-chapter to get underway.

Soon my best friend since kindergarten came to visit and asked for a golf lesson. At the Torrey Pines driving range, equipped with clubs and samurai sword, a magical aura suffused us. An inner *golf sensei* taught through me, and my friend began launching beautiful golf shots with every newly centered swing. Dropping to the grass, her feet and 7-iron in the air, she yelped, "This is like enlightenment! You've got to teach this stuff to the world."

Waves of innate intelligence were spiraling and sweeping past elements of my life into the present. As my golfer-self engaged riches from Aikido and mind-body psychology, integrative flows into the future began emerging. Completely unforeseen, my next career moves and mission were born: developing KiAi Golf and The Centered Way. I became an LPGA Teaching Pro and converted quitting in pain after five holes into Golf BLISS Fitness, playing 100-Hole Charity Marathons, and winning gold medals in the international Jewish Olympics. As if by magic, corporate speaking and coaching opportunities appeared, and adrenal collapse evolved into Stress Less/Prosper More peak performance trainings. I married a woman from Jerusalem and returned to Middle East reconciliation work through joint Israeli-Palestinian Aikido, sports, and healing projects.

What are the chances, and who could think up such things? With my systems back online, I got busy again, but this time I was devoted to living centered and in balance. It's always an imperfect process. Incredibly, my life's work turns out to be teaching and loving what I keep on needing to learn.

A golf student once told me with a wise wonderful grin: *Good or bad, I forgive myself every shot.* We are all on a long winding road, naturally full of peaks and valleys. What if nothing is actually wrong? Life's energy is always here to buoy us up, and divine light is guiding our way if we can only recognize it.

Just four days before his passing from AIDS, I was outside with my head in the lap of my brother's beloved partner as he sat glowing in the sunlight and said:

I have seen the face of God, and it is all our faces. Whether I live or die, it is all a miracle!

Even in the dark, may you keep on the lookout for the magic of wild synchronicities, compassion, and love to give you strength, hope, and the knowing that your next greatest good is surely coming.

Jamie Leno Zimron is a 6th Degree Aikido Black Belt, LPGA Pro, Marriage Family Therapist, Executive Coach, Body-Mind Fitness Trainer, and Citizen's Diplomat. A pioneer in holistic leadership, peak performance, and peace-building, she is creator of The Centered Way and KiAi Golf and co-founder of the Association of Women Martial Arts Instructors and Middle East Aikido Peace Project. Jamie Sensei is an author, Institute for Personal Change facilitator, and Vistage International speaker, teaching and speaking worldwide. Email Jamie at: Jamie@TheCenteredWay.com. Facebook and Linked In: Jamie Leno Zimron

CHAPTER 41

The Unexpected Gift

Mary L. Zozaya

Alone. My arms wrapped around myself as I stared into the dark night. Sleep, which had been my escape and sanctuary, was now elusive. I had moved into the house the week before. It had only taken three months from when he said, "I'm done," to divide the belongings and the assets, pack up, and move. My daughter was at her father's, and I was alone. In the distance, I saw the city and car lights and wondered: *Who is driving at this hour? Are they alone, their family torn apart like mine?*

I couldn't escape this emotional pain, especially in the quiet of the night. During the day, I kept busy, mask in place, completing the tasks, and attending to my responsibilities. I had become very good at this, so good that I was on automatic pilot and had fallen asleep at the wheel of my own life. The shame and the inner critic had taken residence and were inescapable. I was filled with self-doubt and unsure of how to carry on.

My daughter spent every other week with me. In quiet moments when she was away, the past came barreling into my thoughts, seemingly uninvited. I'd like to think they were meant to help me make sense of recent events and help me move through the emotions of anger, loss, grief, but at the time, it felt like a tortuous reliving of traumatic events from my past.

I recall being in church with my dad and my younger sister when I was seven. My mom and our unborn sibling were there, too, but they were in the casket. It seemed everyone in the small farming community had come to the funeral. Stone-like faces were captured in the pictures. Dad lifted me up so I could give Mom one last kiss before she was taken to the hearse. It was an hour-long journey to the cemetery we would visit for the years that followed.

Then it was back to school, farming chores, and the monotony of getting through each day. The pain of separation from Mom felt unbearable. I begged for relief by asking God to take me too. It was not to be because I woke up the next day, and the next day, and the next—doomed to repeat it all again. It was during one of these times of absolute despair in my conversations with God that I received an answer that stopped the begging: *No, you belong here. You have things to do.* It would be years before I would acknowledge this, but at the time, it was enough.

Religion was a large part of my upbringing—rosary every night, Sunday mass, eucharist, confession, and penance. *Marriage.* The sacraments are sacred. No one in my family had divorced; it wasn't in our vocabulary. So much shame arose in me that it led me to hide what I was going through. Those closest to me knew, my sister and her family, my neighbors, and closest friends. Otherwise, it was my dirty secret. In fact, even five years later, I would run into people in my town who were shocked to hear of my divorce.

Shame has a way of gathering steam and momentum if it isn't faced head on and spoken about in order to dissolve its hold on us. Shame, like religion, had a strong presence in my upbringing. We were frequently counseled to do good in school, respect our elders, and not bring shame on the family name. However, the truth was I was ashamed of my family and myself in childhood. We were immigrants, which was just one of the many ways we were different. I had entered kindergarten as a non-English speaker; I couldn't communicate with my teacher and classmates.

In first grade, Mom had died, and Dad was a single parent. I also had unruly curly hair that went in every direction and looked unkept. At a time when it feels safer to fit in, I grew in my insecurities and turned inward. Today, I would tell that girl: *It will all be okay; your uniqueness is a gift you will one day appreciate.*

Looking out again at the dark night in my new house, I realized this time in my life called for courage. I thought of my father who had been born in 1921 in the Basque region of Spain and had endured the Spanish Civil War and World War II. He would tell us how fortunate we were and, to make his point, would describe the horrors of war he had witnessed and what he had to do to survive. Like his two older brothers, when he had the chance to come to North America as an indentured servant, he took it. He left all he knew and loved—without knowing what was ahead—with a conviction that he needed to look for a better way.

My father had dreamed big. He set goals for himself and had a strong commitment to give his family a better life. Each day he toiled the land, planted seeds, harvested the crops, raised farm animals, and provided for his family. He didn't speak English well and had but a second-grade education. However, he had a strong work ethic and fierce dedication to do what it took to provide for his family. I could now see he modeled strength and perseverance. As I stood in the dark, I claimed this lineage with pride rather than shame and realized that this fortitude to carry on during difficult times was in me too. Hiding and allowing emotions to overwhelm and paralyze me was not an option.

Like my seven-year-old self, I once again looked to my faith and asked for guidance. By acknowledging how lost I felt, I provided an opening for a series of unexpected events and people to show up in my life. I was reminded there was a purpose to it all and to let go of how I thought things should be, and I embraced what was unfolding.

I was introduced to meditation, mindfulness, mirror work, visualization, intention setting, a universal spirituality, and so much more. It was a time of trying new things, creating new habits, and staying curious and open to possibilities. Many of these tools are simple practices and yet so difficult to do consistently.

I will share a few in case they might be transformational for you too.

One of the hardest exercises was to look into my eyes in the mirror and tell myself: *I love you*. The words got caught in my throat; I couldn't even choke them out as I was overcome with tears. My internal dialogue was not loving, and I was filled with self-loathing. It took time to be able to do this exercise and mean it. One of the fundamental changes that occurred that made this easier was to redefine my sense of self. Practicing self-love, compassion, and grace is part of my daily intentions.

As my self-love grew, so did my self-care. Instead of hiding and withdrawing, I leaned on my family and friends who always made it a priority to check in on me and be with me whenever I asked. I mindfully chose nourishing food. I resumed playing racquetball and worked on keeping a strong body to care for myself, my daughter, and our home. The exercise also helped me manage stress. I prioritized a healthy sleep routine so that I felt rested and ready for each day.

I saw a counselor for help adjusting to the divorce. I faced my tendencies towards perfection and feeling like a failure. These sessions helped me move through my emotions in a constructive way as I learned to let go of the dreams and aspirations I attached to the marriage.

Today, I begin my day with gratitude, appreciating the beauty in my world. This brings a smile to my face and sets the mood for the day. Through a daily meditation practice, I am gaining awareness of my thoughts and emotions. This allows me to be selective about how I want to show up in the world. I use affirmations, such as: *Every day, and in every way, I get better and better*, and I post positive sayings throughout my home.

By managing the internal dialogue and recognizing the power of words, you can intentionally create positive energy within and through you. This impacts every interaction and experience; there is science to support this. Although our emotions are reactive, you can decide the meaning you attach to events and experiences. You are not defined by your experiences.

One of the unexpected gifts of the divorce has been reflecting on influential times in my life and seeing how they helped prepare me for today. Tonight, I no longer have my arms wrapped around myself protectively. As I look out into the darkness, I notice there is a bright full moon, and I see my own bright light reflected in it. A smile rests on my face, and I feel a sense of joy and wonder. Where there was despair and fear, now hope and gratitude reside.

The telling of this story is one more act of courage for me, of breaking the bonds of shame. What I had perceived as devastating and shameful has been transformed into a positive life-altering experience. I hope the telling of this story offers hope to you if you find yourself reeling from a turning point in your life. I can honestly say that I find joy daily, and amazing opportunities continue to appear. May love fill your heart and hope fill your mind.

Thriving is possible.

Mary L. Zozaya is board certified as a Family Nurse Practitioner, Integrative Nurse Coach, and Lifestyle Medicine Practitioner, and holds a master's degree in Healthcare Administration. During her four decades in healthcare, Mary has had a front row seat to the suffering and triumph of the human spirit. Her greatest delight comes from supporting others as they awaken their own potential and create a joy-filled life. This chapter is her first published work. She can be reached at: mary@blissassociates.net

FINAL THOUGHTS

The writers in this anthology have bared their souls for us, sharing their most difficult moments and deepest insights. They have gifted us with wisdom for what we face today and for what lies ahead. In story after story, they have shared the moments and events that *turned* their lives in a different direction and reshaped them from that point forward.

Have you identified your own *turning point moments*?

Most of the time, we never see the curve in the road ahead until we are navigating it, hands clutching the steering wheel. It is easy to feel isolated and alone when facing these events, but after reading the dozens of stories in *Turning Point Moments*, you can be assured that you are not alone at all. We share similar journeys of pain and loss, of hope and new life. The writers in these pages have offered you the gems of their own experience to carry with you for just such times.

Our publishing team has been personally blessed by each story, each moment, and each act of courage demonstrated by these ordinary people who pushed through their struggles in extraordinary ways. We are inspired to live out their hope in the twists and turns of our own lives, and we know you are inspired as well.

Perhaps one or two stories stood out for you. Many of our authors have included contact information for you to share your story or to inquire about the guidance they offer through coaching, courses, and books. If their message resonates with you, we encourage you to seek out their assistance through their services and products.

As you move forward, we invite you to look for others who are struggling in their own *turning point moments* and ask yourself if your story, your experience, and your wisdom could be a gift for them in their travels. Perhaps you, too, have a gem to share that could make all the difference in someone's world.

Thank you for reading our book and for joining us in our efforts to support each other in these challenging times as we create a better world for us all.

BECOME A CONTRIBUTING AUTHOR

Do you have a *Turning Point Moment* to share with others?
Contribute your story to the next volume:

Turning Point Moments:
True Inspirational Stories About Creating a Life that Works for You
Volume Two

Be one of the first aspiring authors to receive a special invitation
about sharing your story in our next book.

Join our VIP Notification List Now:
www.turningpointmoments.com/volume2

DO YOU HAVE AN IDEA FOR A BOOK?

If reading these stories has inspired you to write your own book, we've got the perfect way to get started.

Our award-winning *Get Your Book Done* program has helped more than 1,000 authors in 47 countries get their book idea out of their head, onto the page, and into the world. Now it's your turn, and you can get started right now, for *free*.

Get Free Help to Write Your Book:
www.turningpointmoments.com/writemybook

NEED HELP PUBLISHING YOUR BOOK?

If you're nearly done, or already finished writing your manuscript and trying to figure out how to get your book published, we're here to help.

Capucia Publishing has been supporting authors to publish life-changing, transformational books since 2004. We're an independent author-centric publishing company with a dedicated team ready to walk you through every single step to seeing your book published and launched into the world. Our comprehensive done-for-you service easily makes your book idea a published reality.

Let's Talk About Publishing:
www.turningpointmoments.com/publish

Connect with Us

Websites
www.turningpointmoments.com
www.getyourbookdone.com
www.capuciapublishing.com

Social Media
f www.getyourbookdone.com/community
@ @christinekloser
in @christinekloser

Mail
Capucia LLC
211 Pauline Drive #513
York, PA 17402

Contact
Phone: (800) 930-3713
Email: support@getyourbookdone.com

Made in the USA
Las Vegas, NV
04 July 2022

51068674R10154